Gadsby's Tavern (1752)
Alexandria, Virginia

Beneath a beautifully detailed cornice and unusual vermiculated keystones, the doorway and windows with their bull-nosed sills and stone lintels are placed with fine symmetry. The brick water-table and the Flemish bond pattern of the facade are typical of many buildings of the period. This is probably the finest inn, from an architectural standpoint, built in Colonial times.

ALEXANDRIA HOUSES

1750~1830

By · DEERING · DAVIS · A · I · D ·
STEPHEN · P · DORSEY · &
RALPH · COLE · HALL

Special article by
NANCY · McCLELLAND · A · I · D ·

BONANZA BOOKS · NEW YORK

INTRODUCTORY NOTE

WITH THEIR CHARACTERISTIC optimism, Americans seem to have taken it for granted that our Colonial and early Federal buildings would largely take care of themselves. Because of the honest and sturdy loveliness built into them by those who were building a nation, and because we have been able to keep wars at a distance, many such buildings still stand—still in use—still beautiful—still tangible links with their builders—still valuable lessons in planning for enduring charm and utility. But meanwhile, the most destructive of all wars has come and gone and our own old buildings are now a tragically larger share of the architectural heritage of mankind. So it is of more than national importance now that we preserve and restore what we have, and it was to that end that we undertook this book and its predecessor on Georgetown.

As to that part of our architectural heritage, still standing in and around Washington, the chances of stimulating renewed interest seemed especially favorable. Great numbers of people had been drawn to the capital by the war and had come into frequent contact with our architectural past. They would, we reasoned, wish to share their enjoyment with friends and relatives at home and would value for themselves, some permanent record of what they had seen. And so it worked out. For this present book on Alexandria, we could scarcely hope for a reception, more cordial than that accorded to its predecessor.

Alexandria, you remember, was the home town of George Washington—of "Lighthorse" Harry Lee—of Robert E. Lee—of many families whose achievements are written imperishably into American history. History was made in its old buildings. So, much patient research went into digging out and verifying stories about those who lived and visited in them. But, disregarding historical associations, these lovely old buildings have practical lessons for Americans who are building today. Through conjectured restoration renderings (most carefully verified), through plans, through architectural details and above all, through selected pictures, we have tried to show them to readers, just as we have, so often, shown them to friends visiting in Washington. There are exteriors, architectural details, interiors with furniture of the period, properly arranged, wall treatments (including authentic wall papers), window draperies and floor coverings—everything in fact which might remind us that, while our future can be whatever we choose to make it, we also have a past of great beauty and distinction.

Along with maps showing the old town at various stages of its development, we thought it worth while to include a list of structures built in the years from 1750 to 1830 and still standing in Alexandria. In attempting such a list, we knew that there might be omissions or an occasional date which some reader might question, but the list should be helpful to such readers as might have opportunity for a personal visit—and so we risked it.

And now—a few words of appreciation. Our thanks are due, above all, to the owners of the houses shown—to the librarians who aided so greatly in collecting the material, whether historical or pictorial—notably to Miss Virginia Daiker, Mrs. C. Denman, Mrs. Clara E. Le-Gear, Mr. William H. Koppy and to Mr. Hugh Clark, all of the Library of Congress, to Miss Mercedes Jordan of the K Street Library, and to Mrs. James Scott and Miss Ellen Burke of the Alexandria Library—to Evelyn Davis and to Miss Mary Dorsey, whose unfailing patience, humor and good judgment transformed our rough notes into printable form—to Police Chief Edgar Simms and to Martin E. Greene and Lillian S. Ellmore of the Alexandria Chamber of Commerce—to Mr. Charles C. Wall, Superintendent of Mount Vernon and his assistant, Mr. Worth Bailey. Mr. and Mrs. Bailey and Mr. and Mrs. Mangum Weeks made contributions, both oral and written, which are highlights of the volume.

DEERING DAVIS
STEPHEN PALMER DORSEY
RALPH COLE HALL

And finally, before we visit old Alexandria together, introductions seem in order. Your guides will be:

DEERING DAVIS, A.I.D.—at present with the Civilian Production Administration—responsible for much of the historical research—the articles on Maps, Washington's Town House and Mount Vernon, this last chapter bringing together many heretofore little known facts concerning the evolution of that lovely plantation house.

STEPHEN PALMER DORSEY—at present an officer of the Department of State—responsible for the chapters on Alexandria's history and architecture, for the list of structures still standing and for most of the stories about the individual buildings.

COMMANDER RALPH COLE HALL, USNR.—formerly an architect in Saint Louis; currently in the Department of State. Commander Hall, having an interest of long standing in the early houses of the new Republic, served as architectural counsellor for this work.

ED. NOTE.

TABLE OF CONTENTS

LIST OF ILLUSTRATIONS

HISTORY OF ALEXANDRIA

ALEXANDRIA CAME INTO actual being as a town on the morning of July 13, 1749, by the public sale of thirty-one lots at an average price of nineteen and a half pistoles (about twenty dollars). The new town was named after John Alexander, who had, in 1670 bought the land from Robert Howsing, the original patentee, for 600 pounds of tobacco. The boundaries and streets were established by John West, the County Surveyor, and amongst those assisting him there was a youth of seventeen, George Washington, by name. Thus began that lifelong association between the town and the man who was destined to bring it deathless fame.

But in 1749, if the town was new, the place was by no means unexplored or unknown. In fact it already possessed quite a respectable history. In 1608 Captain John Smith in pushing up the Potomac as far north as its Falls had found a strip of territory along its south shore between Chesapeake Bay and the Falls which the Indians called Chickawane. In 1645 the area became part of Northumberland—later divided into many counties—and was gradually opened to settlement. In 1669 Governor Berkeley issued a patent for 6000 acres there to Robert Howsing who sold the land, including the future site of Alexandria, to John Alexander in the following year. For some twenty-five years the Indians made life hazardous for settlers in the region and it was not until after the turn of the century that plantation life in the Chickawane area began to assume a more even and settled tenor. Homes and outbuildings were erected, the lands planted in tobacco and ancient Indian trails converted into rolling roads on which the hogsheads of tobacco were rolled to points along the river where the leaf could be inspected, stored and shipped.

In 1732 the General Assembly authorized the building of a warehouse on the Potomac on the upperside of Great Hunting Creek and in 1740 a public ferry came into being at this point—a link in the King's Highway, the principal post road between the North and the South. Several Scottish merchants, among them William Ramsay and John Carlyle who were agents of Glasgow firms, moved up from Dumfries, Virginia, and the community of Bellhaven, named for a well-loved countryman, began to assume importance as a shipping point.

Renamed Alexandria, the town was formally authorized by the Act of 1748, which named as directors and trustees for its building and maintenance, Thomas Lord Fairfax, the Honorable William and George Fairfax, Lawrence Washington, William Ramsay, John Carlyle, Richard Osborne, John Pagan, Hugh West and Gerard and Phillip Alexander. The trustees met monthly, and the minutes of their meetings from 1749 to 1767, which are still extant, recount the town's resurvey in 1753, reservation of lots for a market square, court house and prison, the building of docks and warehouses and the naming of the streets. Those running North and South were Water, Main (later Fairfax), Royal and Pitt—the western boundary of the town, and Duke, Prince, King, Cameron, Queen, Princess and Orinoko running East and West. All of the available lots were built upon by 1762, and the town's limits were extended to provide new building sites. On the petition of the inhabitants, the county records and jail were moved from Fairfax Courthouse to Alexandria in 1752, and in 1769 a Town House was erected from the proceeds of a lottery and public subscription encouraged in part by the dispensation to the public of free rum punch—according to the records "for treat."

While tobacco was the most important product of the surrounding countryside, wheat and corn were raised in quantity and a very considerable trade developed with the mother country and with the West Indies. As early as 1748 a Virginia law provided for the inspection of flour intended for export to insure its cleanliness and purity, and by 1781 Alexandria was first on the flour inspection list. The flour mills established on nearby streams helped bring about the prosperity that built many of the fine town houses which still survive. The tobacco trade kept pace with grain and as a wholesale and shipping center, Alexandria became the terminus of "great and direct roads leading from Vestal's and William's gaps—from the north western parts of the colony" over which great numbers of wagons brought in agricultural products and returned with varied merchandise from abroad.

It is only natural that the focal points of town life became the market and the wharves. In the market square fairs, political and other assemblies were held and produce of all kinds sold. On court days farmers brought over horses, cattle, pigs and poultry from the Maryland shore to trade with their Virginia neighbors. On the water front not only were ships from far quarters to be seen loading and unloading, but here the river fisherman's smaller craft put in, and here stood the ship wrights yard—on water deep enough to launch a ship of any size. An act of 1752 provided for fairs to be held at Alexandria each May and October for the promotion of trade of every port. Those who came to buy and sell found hospitality in taverns or ordinaries where the local citizenry enjoyed themselves with dinners, balls and card playing. The Royal George and the City Tavern—later Gadsbys—were two of the first and best known. Other Eighteenth Century hostelries included the Red Lion, the Bunch of Grapes, the Indian King, and the Rainbow Inn—this last being the headquarters of the drovers and peddlers who carried on their affairs in Sharpshin alley and the horse market.

Eighteenth Century Alexandria, near the frontier, was full of the crude and lusty color of the era. Until 1773 pigs and geese ran at large in the streets. In the jail yard as at Williamsburg, stood the whipping post and the pillory. An English Magazine of 1768 describes the execution at Alexandria of certain slaves who had poisoned their masters and the display of their heads on pikes placed on the chimneys of the jail and courthouse—as at an earlier day on Temple Bar and London Bridge. The Maryland Gazette in 1761 describes the installation of the first mayor in these glowing terms:

"There was held for the first time at Alexandria on St. Andrew's Day the election of Lord Mayor, Aldermen and Council of this city. The Recorder of office was conferred on James Lowrie, M.D. Mr. William Ramsay, first projector and founder of this promising city, was invested with a gold chain and medal. Upon one side was represented the infant state of Alexandria, and its commodious harbor with these words in the legend: 'Alexandria Translate and Benate Auspice Deo,' and in the exergue 'Condita Regn. Geo. II Anno Dom. 1749.'——

The election being ended, the Lord Mayor and Common Council, preceded by officers of State, Sword and Mace bearers, and accompanied by many gentlemen of the town and county made a grand procession to different quarters of the city, with drums, trumpets, a band of music and colors flying.

The company wore blue sashes and crosses in compliment of the day (St. Andrew's) and upon the whole, made a fine appearance. Crowds of spectators followed, many on horseback, and many got on the tops of houses. Loud acclamation resounded from every mouth, and a general joy sparkled in every face. The shipping in the harbor displayed their flags and streamers, continuing firing guns the whole afternoon. A very elegant entertainment was prepared at the Coffee House, where the Lord Mayor, Aldermen and Common Council dined. In the evening a ball was given by the Scots gentlemen, at which a numerous and brilliant company of ladies danced. The night concluded with bonfires, illuminations and other demonstrations."

The Scottish merchants who formed a large percentage of the town's early population naturally exerted a strong influence upon it. The Carlyle House built in 1752 out of the profitable trade of the firm of Carlyle and Dalton, became a meeting place for those of power and influence in the locality. The second floor of the Town House was used for Presbyterian services as well as public assemblies until the old Presbyterian Meeting House was erected in 1774. The ground floor of the same building housed the Alexandria school until it became the Academy.

Many of Alexandria's founders bore names that have become a source of deep pride to Virginians—indeed to all Americans. Washingtons, Fairfaxes, Lees, Custises, Fitzhughs, Alexanders, one of whom later became Earl of Sterling, Masons, Ramseys, Carlyles and many others passed on a tradition of honorable success which, as much as their gracious old homes, gives to present day Alexandria its unique charm. Such names as George Mason, Light Horse Harry Lee and Robert E. Lee will live on as long as the city stands. Any student of Alexandria's history at some point inevitably stops short at the constant repetition of the name of Washington. Yet that is natural and inevitable in the light of the lifelong and intimate association of "the father of his country" with what was in the truest sense of the word, his "home town." He had helped survey it and later was one of its trustees. He owned two lots there as early as 1763, attended Christ Church and was master of the Masonic Lodge. An organizer of Alexandria's first fire company and public school, he was a patron of the Bank of Alexandria and founder and first president of the Potomac Company formed to link the Ohio and Potomac Rivers and promote westward expansion. Small wonder that little can be said of Alexandria without mentioning Washington!

Like Georgetown, five miles to the north, Alexandria has played a notable war role in its two centuries of existence. It was born during the wars with France, and five years after its founding the depredations of the French and their Indian Allies on the western borders of the Colony and in Pennsylvania, forced the crown to fortify the forks of the Ohio. However, Fort Necessity fell to the French, and Washington, then in command of the Virginia Rangers, was sent in 1754 to Fort Duquesne, as it had been renamed, to parley with the enemy. Unsuccessful, he returned to Alexandria and retired to "Mount Vernon." However, in February of the next year, General Braddock, a gallant and experienced commander, arrived at Williamsburg with two regiments of the line. From the Governor's Palace he called a conference of the Colonial Governors of Virginia, Maryland, Massachusetts, New York and Pennsylvania to consider the plan of campaign and the raising of monies to defray its cost. Commodore Keppel proceeded to Alexandria with HMS SEA HORSE and HMS NIGHTINGALE and on the General's invitation Washington resumed command of his militia companies.

Colonel Halket's and Colonel Dunbar's regiments of foot encamped northwest of the town while the Colonial Militia which was quartered in the jail drilled on the market square opposite the City Tavern. On the 20th of April 1755, the Army moved out of the town and action was joined on the ninth of July. Braddock's insistence on meeting an elusive Indian enemy according to the parade-ground principles of contemporary European warfare resulted in his own death and heavy losses not only to the regulars but to the Colonials as well. Of the three companies from the Alexandria neighborhood only thirty odd men returned—a crushing blow to the little city. The following August, Washington was commissioned as Commander of the Sixteen Virginia companies raised to drive out the French, and the market square again saw the militia companies march and countermarch.

But, terrible as were the consequences of his military mistakes, Braddock had, before setting out to keep his rendezvous with death sent a dispatch to London which was destined to have even more far reaching consequences. At the conclusion of the Governor's Conference he wrote, "I cannot but take the liberty to represent to you the necessity of laying a tax upon all his Majesty's dominions in America, agreeably to the result of Council for reimbursing the great sums that must be advanced for the service and interest of the Colonies in this important crisis." A decade later came the hated stamp act and ultimately the revolution. And so it is Carlyle House—meeting place of the Governor's Conference—which is considered by many to be the real birthplace of the American Revolution.

The years following the Stamp Act were turbulent ones for Virginia as the spirit of resistance increased with each Colonial measure of Parliament at home. Patrick Henry's five resolutions introduced before the House of Burgesses on May 29, 1765, clearly presented the case against the home government. In 1770 the protest in the House was so great that Governor Botetourt dissolved the assembly which immediately reconvened at the Raleigh Tavern in Williamsburg. Here George Washington and George Mason brought forward the draft of a paper which formed the basis of the Non-Importation Resolutions. In 1774 Washington presided at the Alexandria meeting to elect delegates to the first Virginia Convention and to protest against the Boston Port Bill. The Fairfax Resolves drawn by George Mason of Gunston Hall and clearly setting forth local reaction to taxation, Parliament and the Crown were presented to the Convention by Washington with the declaration that he was prepared to raise, arm and equip a thousand men at his own expense.

Washington was elected a delegate from Virginia to the first Continental Congress at Philadelphia and on June 15th, 1775, was appointed Commander in Chief of the Continental Army. To his fellow militia officers he wrote from Philadelphia June 30, 1775:

> "Gentlemen: I am now about to bid adieu to the companies under your respective commands, at least for a while. I have launched out into a wide and extensive field—too boundless for my abilities, and far—very far beyond my experience. I am called by the unanimous voice of the Colonies to the Command of the Continental Army—an honor I did not aspire to—an honor I was solicitous to avoid, upon a full conviction of my inadequacy to the importance of the office. **** I shall beg of you—before I go—by no means to relax the discipline of your respective companies.
>
> (signed) G. Washington"

From the Alexandria Independent Companies came this reply—"We are to inform you, Sir, by desire of the Company that if at any time you will judge it expedient for them to join the troops at Cambridge, or to march elsewhere, they will cheerfully do it." The town built armed galleys for the defense of the Potomac and raised more militia. Alexandria men were with their great townsman throughout the long war. They were at Trenton with him, at Valley Forge and Yorktown and at Annapolis when he bade the armies farewell. Alexandria gave the Army of the Revolution many able officers, and the first roster of the Society of the Cincinnati carries nine Alexandria names.

After the Revolution came a period of marked advancement. In 1779 Alexandria was incorporated as a town and divided into wards. In 1785 its limits were further extended one mile west of the market square, southward to Hunting Creek and on the north to Four Mile Run. At the same time Washington Street was graded and paved with stone, sidewalks were laid and oil lamps placed at every street corner. A Committee on Streets was appointed, a watchman, or crier, for each ward was selected, and residents were requested to keep their sidewalks clear of litter. In 1783 a Masonic Lodge was organized, and in 1784 the Alexandria Gazette was founded—now the oldest paper in continuous existence in the country. The Academy was incorporated in 1786 as the first free school in Northern Virginia and was housed in a new building. In 1792 the Bank of Alexandria was founded followed by the Public Library in 1794.

Alexandria became part of the new District of Columbia in 1791 and remained as such until the Act of Retrocession by the Congress, July 9, 1846 returned it to Virginia. During the first decade of its existence as part of the District its population which had numbered only 2,748 in 1790 doubled, and by 1800 its merchants and shopkeepers numbered some 260. There were thirty-four licensed taverns, over 165 drays and carts, ninety-seven pleasure carriages, five tobacco warehouses, five bakeries and a brewery, and four banks were incorporated with an aggregate capital of $600,419. At the beginning of the Nineteenth Century, this town probably consisted of about eight hundred buildings of which many are still standing—making her the richest of Virginia cities in Eighteenth Century structures still extant.

When the British invaded the new Capital City by water in 1814, Alexandria lay directly in the route of the enemy. Fort Washington across the river was abandoned without resistance, and the Corporation had no alternative but to send a committee with a white flag to

Admiral Cockburn whose squadron was drawn up to command the town. There were two frigates, the SEA HORSE of thirty-eight guns and the EURALYUS of thirty-six, two rocket ships carrying twelve guns each and a schooner of two guns. While a contemporary propagandist bewailed the indiscriminate plunder of the enemy and the degrading and humiliating terms of capitulation, Colonel Simms, the Mayor at that time, wrote his wife on September 2, 1814 "It is impossible that men under the circumstances could have behaved better than the British while the town was in their power. Not a single inhabitant was insulted nor injured in their persons or homes." Quantities of exportable supplies, of course, were requisitioned and three ships, two brigs and several river craft were taken.

In spite of the war, by 1820 the population had increased to 8,218 which it approximated for the thirty years following, until it jumped to over 12,600 in 1860. During the twenties and thirties the new steamboats plied the river, and in spite of Alexandria's greatest fire in 1824 new enterprises including furniture, broom, pottery, soap and coach factories added to the town's industrial development. Meanwhile the Episcopal Theological Seminary was established in 1823 and a Quaker School in 1825, and two girls seminaries added to the town's reputation as a regional educational center. Following a period of retrocession the pace of progress quickened, and in 1852 Alexandria acquired the status of a city and political independence from its county. With the next three years railroads linked her with Washington and the Blue Ridge, and a new era of prosperity seemed likely in spite of the gathering clouds of war.

Alexandria's heart was with the South, but her situation, due to her proximity to Washington was precarious. It was in Alexandria that the first blood of the war between the States was shed. While the Capital City, which was protected by a large garrison had not been apprehensive for its safety, the almost unanimous Virginia vote for Secession on May 23, 1861, indicated a menacing situation. In order to protect the Navigation of the Potomac, on May 24th Federal troops moved into Alexandria by both land and water. Among them was a young and popular New York Militia Officer, Colonel Ellsworth to whom President Lincoln had become attached. The Colonel entered the Marshall House, a hotel on King Street, and tore down the Confederate Flag flying from its roof. As he descended the stairs he was shot by the innkeeper who was almost immediately felled by one of Ellsworth's men. Ellsworth's Fire Zouaves, many of whom were New York rowdies, had an intense love and respect for their courageous young Colonel, and when they threatened to burn the town of Alexandria had to be kept on board a steamer anchored off shore. Ellsworth's funeral was held in the East Room of the White House and the President drove in the cortege to the station. From the capital sorrow spread in a wave over the Nation as the premonition of war quickened into reality.

When Robert E. Lee, an Alexandrian by closest ties, accepted command of the Confederate Armies, scores of Alexandria men went with him and their beloved South. In the center of present day Washington Street the figure of a Confederate Soldier facing South marks the place from whence 700 men marched away on May 24, 1861—the day of Ellsworth's death —to join the forces of the Confederacy. The Lost Cause remains deep-graven in the hearts and minds of their kinsmen. To their city, however, the war again brought separation from Virginia. In 1863 Alexandria was made capital of the "Restored Government of Virginia" —the Union occupied area. The secessionist town became a mecca for sightseers and the Marshall House was almost torn to pieces by souvenir hunters. Later the old brick town was overwhelmed by the formation and provisioning of a great fleet to move down the water route against Richmond. The wharves were covered with stores, horses and wagons, heavy guns and pontoons—all the equipment of a great offensive army, while the eyes of the inhabitants reflected their hostility as division after division of the Army of the Potomac moved into the surrounding camps. An immense convalescent center was established. The streets were filled with loitering soldiers, drunken and disorderly. These were unhappy days, and yet they had their compensations, for the city escaped the destruction suffered by the rest of Virginia and the evils of Reconstruction.

Yet in the years following the war the port went into decay. The Baltimore and Ohio Railway diverted Alexandria's coal trade and it fell into a dozing existence beside the Potomac that was uninterrupted until 1918 when a World War jarred it into activity. Again Alexandria's sons went forth—this time to return to a city bursting with new inhabitants brought by the war and quickened by the importance of the Capital City across the Potomac. With the growth of the Federal Government in the last decade many members of Washington's increasing official family, charmed by the old town's great beauty brought near by the automobile, came to Alexandria to live. With the advent of the present War it has assumed the appearance of a boom town. To the regular residents were added an army of "war workers" and service personnel drawn by the huge army and navy installations erected between Alexandria and Washington. From the great airport at her side the dun colored transports roar out to every far flung area of war—now so near in hours. Again, although in a different sense than ever in the past, Alexandria feels very close to war, and she has come to realize that she is now in fact an integral part of a great world capital.

But as wars and the years have come and gone, Alexandria has truly been favored by destiny. Wars have left few scars and even the present boundless prosperity has not destroyed her old dwellings or greatly altered her even and pleasant way of life. The mellow bricks, the gardens of magnolia and box, the lovely doorways and sun-touched knockers still suggest the peaceful and gracious living of an earlier and more unhurried day. But this perhaps is her time of greatest danger. Her industries are growing rapidly. A tide of modern apartments crowds in on her wealth of unspoiled early structures from every outskirt. Lafayette's toast is still appropriate—"The City of Alexandria: may her prosperity and happiness more and more realize the fondest wishes of our venerated Washington!" and to it may be added the wish—it could well be Washington's—may she always hold fast to her rich heritage of tradition and beauty.

ARCHITECTURE OF ALEXANDRIA

SIX MILES SOUTH of the sprawling national capital whose brick tentacles stretch out to encircle the countryside, lies Alexandria, rising above the tidewater marshes that hug the Potomac's Southern shore. Behind it, the wide rolling fields of Virginia, lovely in any season, stretch to the Blue Ridge. Alexandria is today a city of over 60,000 inhabitants, vital and living, with foundries, factories, the Naval Torpedo plant and the second largest freight classification yard in the United States. Yet it is far from an ordinary industrial town. Within the Twentieth Century framework of modern production and suburban buildings, stands quietly and with great dignity the heart of Alexandria—an old town which has changed very slowly with the years. Richest city of the middle Eastern seaboard in number of fine old dwellings, home of Washington and many of his closest associates, its great tradition has been kept alive by the descendants of its founders proud of their illustrious heritage. At first predominately a seaport and market town, Alexandria as is indicated elsewhere in this volume, was established according to a formal plan—however unimaginative—with courthouse and market square and a grid of fine broad streets which when lined with dwellings provided open squares of garden plots to the rear. Like the great seaport towns of New England, the wealth of its merchants (and in this case, of course, of the planters who made it their commercial and cultural center) as well as the manual skill of its early joiners and shipwrights provided it with an enviable and unusual architectural inheritance. Oddly enough it is quite different from that of Georgetown, its Maryland sister a few miles to the North, and its junior by two years.

Alexandria's days of glory and hence of her greatest architectural activity were encompassed within the eight decades from 1750 to 1830—that is, they approximated the similar period of greatest prosperity in Georgetown. It was during the first quarter century of the town's existence that Alexandria found her distinctive local idiom and that Alexandrians formed definite tastes in building. While with a few exceptions Georgetown during the last quarter of the Eighteenth Century was building dwellings with a marked "Federal" feeling adopted during the days of the new republic from the more delicate classic designs of the brothers Adam, Alexandria continued as an influential protagonist of the Georgian style typified by two of her finest early structures, the Carlyle House and Gadsby's Tavern.

The development of the Baroque school in the Seventeenth and Eighteenth Centuries on the continent finally resulted in the elaborate and truly French style known as rococo, which swept over the continent but had little fundamental effect on England. There, a rich but highly ordered and individualized version of the Baroque style peculiarly adapted to the taste and living habits of the day was developed. The Regence Period of France was basically similar in design. The adoption of this English Baroque to Colonial conditions may be said to have been the predominating influence on the decorative arts of Eighteenth Century North America.

It is only natural that the way of life in America never approached the magnificence of life in the mother country. This was a new land but recently carved from a wilderness. Inevitably social values differed to some extent, and despite the wealth which developed rapidly from the skill of the colonials both as agriculturists and merchants, it is unfair to compare colonial interiors even of the best type with the finest British Georgian examples built for royalty or the great nobles. Nevertheless the finest American houses are without peer among those of similar type in England. The standard of taste and living among the planters of the South and the great merchants of the North, that is,—the wealthier colonists—was very high and reflected as closely as the difficulties of communication and transportation would allow, the rapidly changing glass of fashion in Europe.

Eighteenth Century religious thought, etiquette, and art were carried out according to well established form and rules. Along with the study of the classics, and the writing of poetry, an interest in the architectural orders was an integral part of the training of the well rounded gentlemen of diverse interests and many talents who epitomized the Eighteenth Century ideal. The publishing of books profusely illustrated with engravings of architectural details based on the works of Palladio, Vignola, Vitruvius and others, catered to the carefully cultivated taste of the gentry—and in the form of simple carpenter's handbooks and guides, to the artisans who served them. The works of William Kent, William Adam and James Gibbs were all used extensively by "undertakers" and architects, both professional and amateur, in Virginia and Maryland as may be seen by comparing the designs in these books with work executed and still extant in this locale.

The master builders, joiners, turners, etc., of that day must not be passed over without credit. These titles in 1750 meant far more than they do today. A long and difficult apprenticeship had to be served and pride of craft was inherent. It was they who translated the general design desires of their clients into the finished state of proper proportion and scale

very much as today a skilled draftsman designer turns out a beautifully detailed set of blueprints from an architect's rough sketches and instructions. The Eighteenth Century craftsman's blueprints probably consisted of ingrained knowledge gained in his apprenticeship, plus rough working drawings and small English books of detail design.

The smaller pre Nineteenth Century dwelling has usually been neglected in favor of Great Georgian Houses by writers on early American architecture. Moreover their design source has been completely overlooked by all but Fiske Kimball in his "Domestic Architecture of the American Colonies and of the Early Republic." A great deal has been written about the wonderful English folios of architectural design as source material for the large estates and the inference implied is that the smaller places were simpler adaptations. These folios were very rare and expensive, quite out of reach of all but a few wealthy aristocrats. Drawing on this page is taken from Joseph Moxon's small pocket size book on bricklaying—London 1700—inexpensive enough to be owned by any competent craftsman. This drawing, plus the folios of details also in pocket size, obviously is the direct design source of the "town" house type so very prevalent from that day to this. Early in the Eighteenth Century William Halfpenny also of London published another inexpensive small book with twenty-seven plates of designs for "Parish Houses and Farm Houses." A study of these drawings will clearly demonstrate the origin of many early American structures of similar size.

Alexandria's devotion to the mid-Georgian ideal, at a time when the greater delicacy of scale and classic precedent that characterized the designs of the brothers Adam, and in America of Asher Benjamin, had taken firm hold in Maryland and in other parts of Virginia, may be seen in the persistence of the heavier more masculine details and the baroque line in her late Eighteenth and even some earlier Nineteenth Century dwellings. While most of these later structures are actually transitional, the strength of the Mid-Georgian as a "hold-over" style gives the unusual quality and much of the great beauty that is characteristic of Alexandria building during her period of prosperity. While the town contains some definite Federal examples—the Lord Fairfax House is notable—there are few Greek Revival Structures—although the Lyceum is one of the finest examples of that popular school in the country.

The general types of plan are few, although a myriad minor variations may be found adapting these to the individual circumstances and requirements of the family for whom the structure was erected. Five principal types of dwelling are characteristic of the local scene. The earliest is the simple one-story and attic rectangular type of frame construction with center entry and twisting stair, and two rooms on the main floor. Examples are found in the Fawcett (page 35) and Ramsay houses. When the occupants outgrew these quarters they were usually enlarged either by the addition of an ell or of two more rooms built across the house at the rear, which necessitated a change of roof line as in the case of the Ramsay house. This form is the direct successor to the earliest Virginia or Maryland plan consisting of one great chamber entered from the center and having fireplaces at each end. The second type in Alexandria, is the "flounder" house of two stories with half a gable roof—that is, a half house formed as if a gabled structure were split down its center. A gallery usually appears at the side, and the house is built some distance from the street with the long wall set on the lot line. It is believed that this unique form originated as a result of the early ordinance requiring that each lot in the new town be built on by the purchaser within a limited time period. As a result a rear wing was erected to validate the deed but the main structure was never constructed.

The third—the Robert E. Lee house is an example—is the large rectangular brick type with center hall and four major ground floor rooms—the second story approximates the first and a dormered attic permits still other smaller chambers. The fourth is the manorial type, such as the Carlyle House or Mount Vernon, flanked by lower identical wings sometimes joined to the main edifice by covered "curtains" or passageways and covering generous plots of ground—essentially a country model. The last—the typical "town house"—is of rectangular or square form with entrance and hall at the side and two chambers opening from it. Usually of brick, although, as in the case of the William Brown House covered with weatherboards, it is of two stories and dormered attic or of three full stories. Both the third and last types discussed above originally housed the kitchen in a separate dependency to the rear. Later these were normally joined to the main house. In the final development a one or two story ell (containing kitchen facilities and servants' quarters) was added to the rear of the main mass.

In the case of frame structure the siding is of great width sometimes graduated as it approaches the roof line—that is, with the widest at the level of the earth (the foundation was frequently covered) and decreasing in size in proportion to the distance from the ground. Either the weatherboards are placed over brick or brick is used as insulation between the studding. Alexandria is primarily a city of brick. Brickwork of the earliest structures is less regular than that of later date. The bricks are of much rougher cast and obviously of hand moulded origin. Rubbed bricks are used to cap and finish the characteristic watertables of the earlier dwellings. Bricks of the Eighteenth Century buildings are larger than those made today and vary from a dull salmon color when clean to chocolate brown when thoroughly covered with decades of dirt and dust. Carefully laid up in Flemish bond and sand moulded by hand, they offer a refreshing contrast to the white stone lintels, sills and wooden trim. The jointing is carefully struck and "rodded" which gives a crisply finished effect to the whole mass. The clean white mortar is made of pulverized oyster shells and white bay sand.

With several exceptions of gambrel and hip types the roofs are of simple gabled form with the pitch becoming less acute toward the end of the first quarter of the Nineteenth Century as the Federal style assumed dominance over the Georgian. The wooden cornices are refined and relatively elaborate, usually with fretwork beneath the lowest moulding and modillions, and frequently run completely around the structure at the level of the front and rear eaves attractively framing the gable ends in pediment form. Chimneys appear in pairs at the roof ends flush with the walls and chimney tops are often moderately shaped. Dormers are gabled, either with a square or circular head upper sash and with supporting pilasters duplicating the treatment of the principal entrance. The fenestration is carefully arranged and windows are usually of twelve lights with six panes in each sash. Muntins and surrounding mouldings in typical Georgian work are bold though simple and become more delicate during the transition period. The average width of the former at the beginning of the period was approximately an inch, but they became sharper and narrower as larger lights were used. Sills are typically of white stone as are the lintels which carry heavy grooved or vermiculated keystones. In the earlier examples strongly shaped quoins of the same material accent the corners of the structure, and stone string courses are also used. Doorways most often are formed with semi-circular heads and fine glass transoms of beautiful design. Typically they are framed in wood—with deep paneled reveals—and fluted pilasters support a hollow denticulated classic pediment with richly ornamented soffit. An emphasized keystone set in the round arch of the transom may repeat those of the windows. Fine wrought iron work of sturdy simple type is occasionally used in handrails. Entrance doors and the heavily louvered blinds were invariably painted dark green with other wood trim white.

It is significant that in the few instances in which an English architect of note made a trip to the Colonies on a specific commission, the entire house was walled, floored and roofed before his arrival, and the interior details of panels, cornices, stairs, chimney pieces plus the exterior trim were the fields to which his attention was limited. In actuality he acted in the capacity often filled today by the interior decorator. When one fashionable English architect was persuaded to do a large Virginia country seat he did not arrive in the colony until the house had been building for four years! Houses of small or medium size preserved much the same appearance for several centuries. Their interiors, both in architectural detail and decorative furnishings display more clearly defined epochs or periods. Thus the interiors of these mid-Georgian examples are of particular significance.

From 1725 until the Revolution, interior woodwork of great elaboration characterized the city dwelling and the large country house and even appeared to a surprising extent in smaller country dwellings. Boldly beveled paneling of stile and rail type was used, often surrounded by bold mouldings and fretwork. In the finer structures full paneled rooms of this type, enriched with pilasters and cyma curved baroque pediments judiciously employed, produced an interior whose beauty no amount of plaster ornamentation, applied cast detail or strict adherence to the usual forms can hope to equal. More often the fireplace wall and chimney piece is paneled in combination with embrasured windows having folding or sliding shutters, paneled seats and a wide dado. While delicate mantelpieces did not appear until after the Revolution, heavily moulded shelves were often incorporated in over-mantel designs. The fireplace is usually surmounted by one large panel or a composition of smaller ones framed by the same "crosetted" corners as the fireplace opening. The latter, faced with plaster over brick, slate, tiles, or marble, grew smaller and more shallow as the century progressed. Sides were canted at more extreme angles to make more efficient heating mechanisms and flues were sufficient but not of a size to waste heat. The chimney piece sometimes is flanked by fluted pilasters whose caps support a pediment complementing those of the over doors.

Cupboards were often employed and developed not only as utility measures but as definite features of the decorative treatment. Doors were most often of six panels frequently beveled on both sides, and in the more elaborate examples such as the parlor at Mount Vernon, were made of polished mahogany. Box locks of brass or iron with brass knobs were employed. At the intersection of wall and ceiling, carefully carved cornices were used, elaborated with dentils, modillions and rosettes. The small front entries and twisting stairs were superseded by wide halls of center or side type which connected the front and rear of the houses and were enriched by pilastered arches with paneled soffits, dados and cornices and featured a graceful flight of broad stairs. Spandrels are of sawn scroll type or richly carved (see below), and balusters and newel posts are carefully turned.   Floors are of wide hard red pine planks oiled and waxed.

Ceilings are plainly plastered and in a few cases employ moulded plaster ornament, and were plainly whitewashed as were the walls above the chair rail or dado—thus providing contrast to the painted woodwork. Fine wall papers of scenic or flock type, printed in squares, were exceedingly popular. Paint colors at first were strong, gradually becoming lighter, un-

Photograph: Library of Congress

The carved spandrel ornaments on this stairway are
unusually interesting.

til at the end of the century pastels—robin's egg blue, gray green, French gray, and light putty vied for position as the most popular tints. Fabrics used principally for drapery and upholstery purposes were silks, brocades and toiles in clear bold colors. Mahogany furniture of Chippendale inspiration, used with "Turkey" carpets and hand tufted rugs from France or England, was succeeded by the Hepplewhite and Sheraton styles and textiles with classic motif. Alexandria-made silver and furniture, (as closely as possible), emulated that imported from England or brought down from Philadelphia, and the sociability of the tea table brought with it fine export porcelain from China and the mother country.

These are the mid-Georgian characteristics most typical of Alexandria. It is true, that in the following pages several classic Federal types are shown in addition to one superb porticoed Greek Revival building, yet they are not quite expressive of true Alexandria idiom. The Federal houses, however, are exquisite in the delicacy of scale and classic ornament that characterizes them as true expressions of the general quality of life and effort in the new Republic. The curved baroque line eventually yields to the straight. Richly carved wood interior trim of masculine proportion gives way to delicate composition. Overmantels and overdoors cease to be. Carved cornices are replaced by brick corbel tables, and pedimented wooden entrances by more severe round or elliptical arched doorways—often with side as well as fan lights. Iron work is used frequently, mouldings become delicate, windows larger and longer, the rough brick smooth—in short the trimness of purest classicism replaces the sturdy beauty of modified baroque.

One who visits Alexandria today will find its houses set close to the brick side walks, but to the rear and at the sides are lovely sheltered gardens shaded by great trees. Here are old smoke houses and stables, arbors of grapes and wisteria, and the dark gloss of magnolia and box picked out by brilliant garden flowers of species that have bloomed here for almost two centuries. The alleys and some of the streets are still cobbled. Those thoroughfares running east reach the river sharply; and between the poplars at the end of Prince Street, the waterfront with its wooden wharves is a reminder of the forgotten importance of Alexandria as a port. Throughout this fabric runs the red and white masonry of the architecture to which this book is devoted.

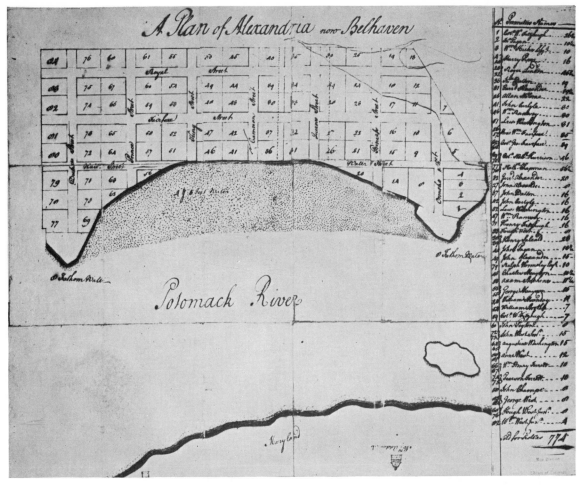

The original official survey plot of Alexandria drawn in 1749 by George Washington at the age of seventeen.

MAPS OF ALEXANDRIA

THE ATTEMPT to verify the building dates of early structures will soon transform the seeker after truth into a confirmed cynic. In most cases generally accepted information will turn out to be mere legend. The facts, when uncovered, will often prove the actual erection time to have been fifty or more years later. In this type of research there seem to be few rules and many exceptions—but here is a helpful generality.

In attempting to establish the dates of the old houses of any city, it is an excellent first step to investigate all successive maps or plats of the community. If a house whose date is desired exists on a lot not shown as part of the town at a given time, it is fair to assume that it may have been erected at a later date. Of course this is not conclusive for in many instances nearby existing farm structures were later included in the limits of an expanding town.

However in any locality, these exceptions obviously would not seriously lessen the value of this first step. But valuable or otherwise, it is not an easy one to take. Search for correct erection dates in Alexandria, for instance, brought to light no less than twenty-two different versions of the town's growth, from 1749 to the Revolution. Finally, after six months of search, Dr. William J. Van Shreeven, Head Archivist of the Virginia State Library, Rich-

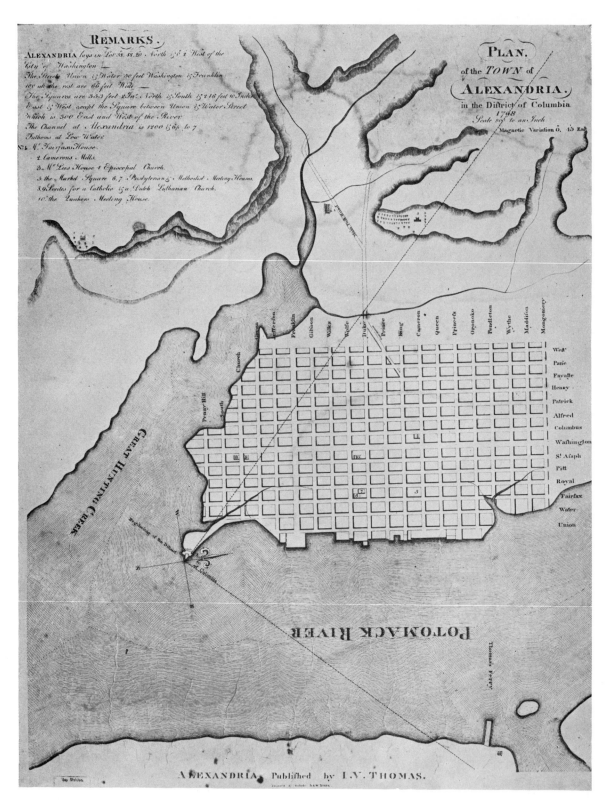

Photograph: Library of Congress

mond, Virginia, was contacted through the kind recommendation of Mr. Thomas T. Waterman. Dr. Van Shreeven provided the reference which gave the location of the one official early addition, made by act of the Virginia Assembly in 1762 (W. W. Henning, Statutes at Large of Virginia, Vol. VII, pages 604-607, the act of November 1762 for enlarging the town of Alexandria).

But even so, the fact that a structure stands on a lot in the original Pre-Revolutionary part of town, or in an authenticated Pre-Revolutionary addition is not conclusive proof that it is of Colonial date. The splitting up of the original half acre Alexandria lots and replacements after fires, etc. must account for many of the structures in this part of the town. Still, an obviously very old house in this area *could* certainly have been built before the Revolution, whereas if an old building is in one of the squares added later, its erection date can not easily be accepted as having been before the addition of that part of the city.

At any rate successive plots afford a valuable check against dates too readily accepted generally and not verified by any positive record and another check is provided by construction methods and features of design and ornamentation. People then were responsive to the dictates of changing fashion, just as they are now. But alas, this rule too has exceptions. Some people then were rugged individualists—just as some people are now. So it boils down to this: Maps can give some check. Prevailing fashions can give some check. But if one wants the actual erection date of some old building, and wants it beyond all contradiction, he must locate some positive record amongst old legal or personal papers.

NOTES ON GILPIN AND HIS MAP OF ALEXANDRIA

The plan of Alexandria on preceding page, is that drawn by Colonel George Gilpin, engraved by Thomas Clarke of New York in 1798, and published by John V. Thomas at Alexandria in 1799. Our illustration is from an impression in the collection of 18th Century maps and engravings owned by Mr. and Mrs. Mangum Weeks of Alexandria. The original copper-plate of this plan, after having been lost for nearly a century and a half, came into the possession of Mr. and Mrs. Weeks who published for subscribers a limited edition in 1944. There is only one known extant impression of an earlier edition of this very rare plan.

Thomas Clarke was a well known engraver who worked in Philadelphia and New York. Dunlap recorded his brief career in his *History of the Rise and Progress of the Arts of Design in the United States* (1834; new ed. 1918, Vol. II, p. 174). John V. Thomas was the publisher of the *Alexandria Advertiser.* On 21 September 1797 he inserted a notice in his newspaper, asking for the return of "a plan of the town of Alexandria neatly drawn by Col. Gilpin" which he had lent to an unrecalled acquaintance; and some two years later, on 4 December 1799, he advertised in the *Time and District of Columbia Advertiser,* that "this day is published . . . . a plan of the town of Alexandria drawn by Col. Gilpin, and handsomely engraved." Thus the plan made its appearance just ten days before General Washington's death at Mount Vernon. Whether he saw the engraved plan or not, he undoubtedly knew the drawing well, for Colonel George Gilpin, its draughtsman, was a resident of Alexandria, intimately associated with Washington. Gilpin had fought in the Revolution and on the organization of the Potomac Company, of which Washington was President, became one of its four Directors. This canal project was to link the Ohio and the Mississippi by water with the Chesapeake, and so to realize Washington's dream of Alexandria as a great deposit for the furs and other produce of the Western Country, a great entrepôt and seaport which would outstrip Philadelphia. Washington's diary and letters contain many references to this scheme which was close to his heart. His letter to Jefferson of 30 May 1787, written on the eve of the Constitutional Convention at Philadelphia, is typical (*See* Washington's Writings, Fitzpatrick's Bicentenary Edition, Vol. 29, page 217). Gilpin's Plan shows the last phase of the 18th Century city, after the enlargement authorized by the General Assembly in 1785.

We have discussed elsewhere the growth of the 18th Century city, but a word may be said here on the historical significance of the names of the streets since they so vividly recall four distinct periods in the town's growth. The original streets testified the loyalty of the city fathers by such names as Royal, King, Queen, Prince, Princess, and Duke. 'Duchess' yielded its logical place to Oronoko, named for an old tobacco landing. The only individual honored was the Proprietary of the Northern Neck, the 6th Lord Fairfax of Cameron, (the patron of the young surveyor Washington), who had been active in founding the town and after whom the principal streets in both the North-South (Fairfax) and East-West (Cameron) axes were named. The next quarter-century's growth reflects the downfall of the French power in America in Wolfe Street, and the rising resistance to English coercion in Pitt, Wilkes and St. Asaph Streets—the last named after the bishop of that See, Dr. Jonathan Shipley, a friend of Dr. Franklin and an outspoken champion of the American cause. The first year of the Revolution saw the publication of the first volume of the *Decline and Fall of the Roman Empire* and the city in her next street, Gibbon, paid tribute to the historian of the great empire of the ancient world even while her own citizens were dissolving their allegiance to the sovereign of the greatest empire of the modern world. Foremost in this struggle stood Washington and Franklin, and to do them pre-eminent honor the city laid out two new streets, half as wide again as any in the old town, each lying in one of the principal axes of the town, Washington running north and south, and Franklin, east and west. The new streets west and south of these, respectively, and north of Oronoko, which were added after 1785, bear the names of military heroes, as Greene, Lafayette and Montgomery, or of rising statesmen, as Henry, Jefferson and Madison. Unlike Georgetown in the nearby Federal City, all the streets today still retain their old names save Water Street which was renamed after Secession, for General Lee.

The growth of Alexandria in area was as follows:

I. The town was created in 1749, by act of Assembly, containing 84 half-acre lots.

II. 1762—Act of Assembly added 57 half-acre lots.

III. 1779—Lots sold privately by J. Alexander prior to 1779 were incorporated at this time.

IV. 1785—The town was greatly enlarged.

V. 1786—A few improved adjacent lots were added. There have been further minor enlargements but Alexandria reached its approximate present size in 1785-6. Inside book covers show the Plot only from the Week's engraving and superimposed on it the 1749 survey and the 1762 addition.

THE DOCTOR DICK AND GEORGE WILLIAM
FAIRFAX HOUSES

209 Prince Street
207 Prince Street

The red brick house (circa 1770) on the left in the following photograph was the home of Dr. Elisha Cullen Dick, for many years noted physician, Health Officer of Alexandria, close friend of Washington. It was he, as one of the attending doctors, who stopped the clock in the first President's bedroom at 10:20 P.M. the moment of his death. A few days later on December 18, 1799, as Washington's successor as Worshipful Master of the Alexandria Lodge of Masons, he conducted the Masonic Service at the funeral. Dr. Dick, who came to Alexandria from Philadelphia, in 1783 and probably purchased the house at that time, had been a member of the Established Church but became a Quaker. At this time he is said to have thrown his dueling pistols into the Potomac from which they were rescued and given to the Masons who now exhibit them in their museum. He died in 1828 and is buried in an unmarked grave in the Quaker cemetery on Queen Street. The residence retains perhaps the finest interior wood work of any Alexandria Colonial dwelling other than the Carlyle House's Blue Room. The vermiculated key stones are reminiscent of Gadsby's.

The adjoining house to the right, with the original color of its old bricks hidden under coats of light colored paint, stands on the lot purchased in 1749 by Colonel William Fairfax of Belvoir, manager of the Virginia holdings of his cousin, Thomas Lord Fairfax. In 1753 he deeded it to his son, George William Fairfax, one of whose sisters married Lawrence Washington and became first mistress of Mount Vernon. George William Fairfax visited England shortly before the Revolution and as a Loyalist never returned to Virginia. The property next passed into the hands of Robert Adam, a wealthy Scot and first Master of the Masonic Lodge. Washington's diary records different occasions on which he went fox hunting and fishing with Adam.

Mrs. Charles Beatty Moore the well-known authority on historic Virginia has beautifully furnished the buff painted structure. The exact building date of this old house has been much argued and, unfortunately, its original interior wood work has disappeared making architectural identification difficult.

209 and 207 Prince Street

The Dr. Dick and George William Fairfax Houses

120 Prince Street, circa 1770
(opposite the Dr. Dick House)

The interior architectural details and furniture are very fine.

Photograph: Library of Congress

213 Prince Street, circa 1760

The dormers and cornice with their thoughtful scale, detail, and design denote a fine example of the Pre-Revolutionary town house.

The interior trim more than fulfills the exterior's promise

THE DENNIS RAMSAY HOUSE
221 South Lee Street

This frame dwelling was built circa 1760 for Colonel Dennis Ramsay, Alexandria's First Mayor and the son of William Ramsay who was instrumental in founding the city. Architecturally it is a fine example of the single "town house" type in wood. 213 Prince Street (page 28) is typical of the same facade in brick. Originally the foundation now exposed was sheathed in wood, even the projecting water table was covered by a strip. Mr. Van Devanter has exercised extreme care and exceptional taste in his selection of furnishings. They are not only beautiful but in proper scale as well.

Hand-reft siding on this house built about 1760 is in the original state

Photograph: Library of Congress

Note the beading and extreme width of these original boards

Photograph: Walter D. Wilcox

A corner chimneypiece of delicate scale complemented by antiques of simple quality

THE FAWCETT HOUSE
Circa 1755
517 Prince Street

This house is a near contemporary of Alexandria's oldest dwelling, the home built in 1748 by William Ramsay, which was recently saved from demolition. Its original center hall plan is indicated by the weatherboards of the facade which were changed with the addition of an entrance porch at the side—not shown in the photograph. The porch, a later addition, is protected by jalousies, and the original structure exhibits wide beaded weatherboards and heavily louvered blinds. The two front rooms of the old house have fireplace walls with simple stile and rail paneling, with raised beveled panels similar to those of contemporary New England country rooms. Although both buildings are reminiscent of similar small dwellings still standing in Williamsburg, details and general plan are not typical of Virginia and other influences undoubtedly contributed to their design.

The original center entrance is discernible on the siding

35

GADSBY'S TAVERN

Circa 1752

132 North Royal Street

In reality two distinct buildings erected forty years apart, this historic edifice was the finest tavern in the Colonies built before 1800. The smaller of the two was built in 1752 as the City Tavern. On three different occasions Washington occupied it as his headquarters and here in 1775 he presided at a meeting which resulted in the adoption of the Fairfax Resolves, drawn by George Mason of nearby Gunston Hall.

Its superiority in the final and double stage is due to the shrewd foresight of John Wise, the proprietor, who ordered the extensive addition to the North in 1790. He rightly foresaw the need for superior accommodations near the new Federal City and on the post road that extended from Williamsburg to Boston. In 1793 the tavern passed into the hands of John Gadsby, an Englishman who owned a coach line jointly with the keepers of The Spread Eagle at Philadelphia and The Swan at Lancaster, and the tavern became the stopping place of many of our own statesmen as well as those from afar en route to visit General Washington at Mount Vernon. In 1824 Lafayette was tendered a banquet at the tavern, where during the Revolution he had met John Paul Jones and Baron deKalb. Here in 1808 Ann Warren, the celebrated English actress died while playing in Alexandria, and here in November 1792 was announced a "meeting of the golf club to be held in their rooms in Gadsby's Hotel!"

The 1792 addition is famous for its great assembly room, and while the original building, because of its size, is not as obviously unusual, no other Inn of its period remains with such thoughtful perfection of simplicity in its architectural detail and in such remarkably unaltered condition. An English Archbishop travelling in Virginia remarked upon the unique fact that such "ordinaries were kept by gentlemen and that only such were entertained." The pride which the founders of Alexandria had in their town, their high hopes for its future, and their wealth and taste all contributed to the tavern's excellence, but to its unknown builder should be ascribed the major credit. The original wooden entrance is the finest in Virginia. The chimney pieces with their mantels and paneling are jewels of simple Georgian design, although the fact that not one of the rooms is fully paneled is disappointing and unusual in a building of this date.

The Ball Room in the older part followed a Scotch precedent and extended across the entire second floor front. A number of Alexandria private dwellings utilized the same plan to create a second floor double parlor on the street front. This feature was unique in this country at that time.

Legend has it that Lord Fairfax imported the bricks for this tavern from England. A similar story of importing English bricks crops up continually in the early architectural history of this country and is based on error. We made excellent bricks ourselves. However, the unusual vermiculated window key stones may well have been of English origin and without doubt the Fairfax family contributed to the cost of construction as did the other prominent Alexandrians of the time. The books of Carlyle and Dalton show that they paid Lamphere, a joiner of Alexandria, for turning the stair rails of the City Tavern. These rails are very like those at Mount Vernon which also were made by Lamphere. Undoubtedly this building must be considered along with Carlyle House and Mount Airy as one of the design influences on young George Washington when the major changes were ordered for Mount Vernon in 1758.

The great assembly room of Gadsby's 1792 addition was the scene of a public dinner for Lafayette in 1824 at which The Honorable John Quincy Adams, Commodores Rogers and Porter and veterans of the Revolution were also present. It is interesting that Robert E. Lee, still only a boy, was a marshal in the procession of Revolutionary veterans and honored guests which preceded the dinner.

Here, too, were held the birth-night balls in honor of Washington who always remained until late hours and thoroughly enjoyed them. His adopted son, George Washington Parke Custis, has left us the following fascinating account.

"The birth-night balls were instituted at the close of the Revolutionary War and its first celebration, we believe, was held in Alexandria. Celebrations of the birth-night soon became general in all the towns and cities, the twenty-second of February, like the Fourth of July, being considered a national festival. In the larger cities, where public balls were customary, the birth-night, in the olden time, as now, was the gala assembly of the season. It was attended by all the beauty and fashion, and at the seat of government, by the foreign ambassadors, and by strangers of distinction. The first president always attended on the birth-night. The etiquette was, not to open the ball until the arrival of him in whose honor it was given; but, so remarkable was the punctuality of Washington in all his engagements, whether for business or pleasure, that he was never waited for a moment in appointments for either. Among the brilliant illustrations of a birth-night of five and thirty years ago, the most unique and imposing was the groups of young and beautiful ladies, wearing in their hair bandeaux or scrolls, having embroidered thereon, in language both ancient and modern, the motto of *Long live the president!*"

"The minuet (now obsolete) for the graceful and elegant dancing of which Washington was conspicuous, in the vice-regal days of Lord Bottourt in Virginia, declined after the Revolution. The commander-in-chief danced, for his last time, a minuet, in 1781, at the ball given in Fredericksburg, in honor of the French and American officers, on their return from the triumphs at Yorktown. The last birth-night attended by the venerable chief was in 1798. Indeed he always appeared greatly to enjoy the gay and festive scene exhibited at the birth-

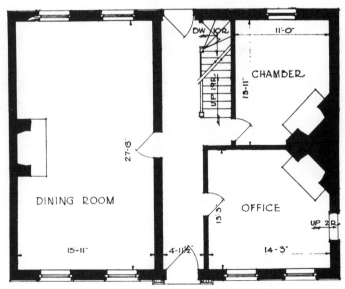

Floor Plan: Library of Congress

The first floor plan of the original tavern

This magnificent doorway is termed the finest one of wood in Virginia. Its fluted Doric pilasters support a superb pediment with dentiled cornice and richly ornamented soffit.

Photograph: Harris & Ewing

The finely turned balusters in the form of Doric columnettes above vase profiles are characteristic of contemporary work farther North.

Fine broken pediment over-door in the Dining Room of the 1752 building

Photograph: Harris & Ewing

Deep paneled reveals are an interesting feature of this opening in the addition's **Parlor**

Photograph: Harris & Ewing

Corner mantel of the simpler type in a ground floor chamber

Ballroom mantelpiece

A duplicate is at the room's opposite end

The scrolled pediment with terminal rosettes, frieze with Doric triglyphs and fluted pilasters give this overmantel unusual distinction.

The Great Assembly Room

The original room of 1793 now in the Metropolitan Museum, has been duplicated in the Tavern as it stands today. Of unusual size, it is a magnificent example of the survival of a style for many years after the date of its greatest popularity. Openings are symmetrically located with walls paneled only to chair rail height, but with wooden chimney breasts from floor to ceiling. Architraves around doors and windows and the panel mouldings are conventional in profile, but a suggestion of the late date of construction may be seen in the tendency toward refinement in these mouldings and in the scale of the cornice and the door heads. The former is enriched by the modillion course with dentils below. Dentil bands in the overdoors are reminiscent of the cornice, and the chair rail carries a band of fret work. The light gray-green color is a reproduction of the original paint, and the hanging balcony for musicians is a charming and unusual feature.

45

The Courtyard

night balls, and usually remained to a late hour, for, remarkable as he was for reserve and the dignified gravity inseparable from his nature, Washington ever looked with most kind and favoring eye, upon the rational and elegant pleasures of life."

The following scene also was described by Mr. Custis. "It was in November of the last days that the General visited Alexandria upon business, and dined with a few friends at the City Hotel. Gadsby, the most accomplished of hosts, requested the General's orders for dinner, promising that there was a good store of canvas-back ducks in the larder. 'Very good, sir,' replied the chief, 'give us some of them, with a chafing-dish, some hominy, and a bottle of good Madeira, and we shall not complain.'" No sooner was it known in town that the General would stay to dinner, than the cry was for the parade of a new company, called the Independent Blues, commanded by Captain Piercy, an officer of the Revolution; the merchant closed his books, the mechanic laid by his tools, the drum and fife went merrily round, and in the least time the Blues had fallen into their ranks and were in full march for the headquarters.

"Meanwhile the General had dined, had given his only toast of 'All our Friends,' and finished his last glass of wine, when an officer of the Blues was introduced, who requested, in the name of Captain Piercy that the Commander-in-Chief would do the Blues the honor to witness a parade of the Corps. The General consented, and repaired to the door of the hotel, looking toward the public square—. The troops went through many evolutions with great spirit, and concluded by firing several volleys. When the parade was ended the General ordered the author—to go to Captain Piercy and express to him the gratification which he, the General, experienced—. Thus the author—had the great honor of hearing the last military order issued in person by the Father of his Country."

The Metropolitan Museum purchased all but a few doors, one damaged mantel, and the floors of the 1792 addition. However, it has been accurately and painstakingly restored through the auspices of the Virginia Chapter of the Daughters of the American Revolution. Thanks are also due to this organization for restoring the original 1752 portion which amazingly remained through all the years in practically original condition though it had been allowed to deteriorate alarmingly. The third building now standing as an extension to the 1790 portion has no historical significance. There were some twelve parts to this famous tavern in 1800 including, stables, coach house, kitchens, etc. The American Legion now owns and operates the buildings as a Museum.

A plate from the folio of James Gibbs published—London—1728

MOUNT AIRY

Mount Airy, one of the finest mid-Georgian country houses now extant in the United States, was completed in 1758 for John Tayloe, wealthy head of that great Virginia family of planters which a generation later built the Octagon as a town house in Washington.

It was undoubtedly the most talked of mansion in Virginia at this time. The unusual design of its curved arcades, the use of dressed stone rather than the almost universal brick plus the prominence of the Tayloe family assured much comment. Surely young George Washington was one of its many admirers and consciously or unconsciously was influenced by it when planning Mount Vernon.

Unfortunately Mount Airy suffered a bitter loss by fire in 1840 when the fine full mahogany paneling which it contained was destroyed. A bit of exquisite cornice mould that was rescued and is now used as a mantel shelf gives one an idea of the departed magnificence of its interior.

It is still owned and occupied by the Tayloe family and consequently is filled with authentic fine silver, portraits, and furniture.

This recent photograph of Mount Airy shows an unusual example of almost literal copying from an English engraving. The connecting passages and pavilions do not appear clearly as they curve towards the opposite facade.

THE CARLYLE HOUSE
123 North Fairfax Street

Over its doorway, the Carlyle House carries a keystone carved with the initials of its builders, John and Sara (Fairfax) Carlyle, and the date of its completion, 1752. John Carlyle, born in Dumfries, Scotland, settled in 1740 at the little town of the same name in Prince William County, Virginia, as agent for a firm of Glasgow merchants. Eight years later he became one of the incorporators of Alexandria. Senior partner of the prosperous firm of Carlyle and Dalton, he married Sara, daughter of the Honorable William Fairfax of Belvoir. Colonel Fairfax, who managed the enormous estate of his cousin, Thomas Lord Fairfax—at one time comprising one-fifth of the present Commonwealth of Virginia—had at various times been Justice of the Bahamas, Governor of the Isle of Providence, and Collector of the Port at Salem in New England. It is not strange that he was one of the first trustees of Alexandria and Collector of Customs on the South Potomac, or that his son-in-law built the most imposing house in the new community.

In 1755 John Carlyle was appointed by Governor Dinwiddie as Major and Commissary of the Virginia militia, and in 1758 he succeeded his father-in-law as Collector of His Majesty's Customs. It was in his house that on April 14, 1755 General Braddock and Commodore Keppel met with Governors Dinwiddie of Virginia, Sharpe of Maryland, Morris of Pennsylvania, DeLancey of New York and Shirley of Massachusetts, to consider the plan for the imminent campaign against the French and Indians along the Ohio River. In view of his experience in dealing with the French the year before, the twenty-three year old militia commander, George Washington, was invited to meet with these distinguished statesmen, who were deeply impressed with his ability and bearing. The recommendation of the council that a tax be levied on the Colonies to defray the many expenses of defense against the French and Indians, when finally carried out ten years later, resulted in the resistance of the Colonies, the Declaration of Independence in 1755 and the eventual establishment of the United States.

Colonel Carlyle, who cast his lot with the Colonies, died in 1780, and was buried in the old Presbyterian cemetery on Fairfax Street. His only son, George William, was killed at the battle of Eutaw Springs September 8, 1781 while serving under Light-Horse Harry Lee. The importance of the Carlyle House as the political and social center of Alexandria, however, was undiminished for many years, and among many other great names of American history identified with its guests, are Franklin, Lafayette, Light-Horse Harry Lee, Mason, Marshall, Jefferson, Charles Carroll of Carrolton and John Paul Jones.

Yet, more impressive than its historical significance is its architectural importance as one of the great houses of Virginia. Of formal plan, the central mass was erected about seventy-five feet to the rear of Fairfax Street with flanking pavilions placed approximately on the present building line. The West or entrance facade had a handsome gate leading to a flagged terrace with retaining wall. The conjectured restoration drawing by Deering Davis, (page

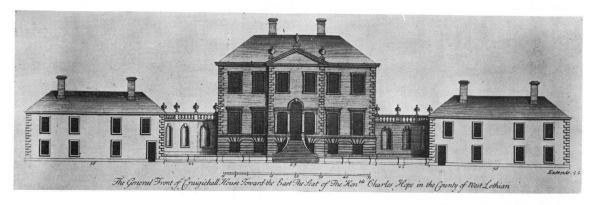

A plate from Vitruvius Scoticus, a folio of engravings—London circa 1730—depicting the architectural works of William Adam.

51) shows no connecting arcades. These were undoubtedly planned though local history denies their actual erection. Today hidden behind an apartment house and with its wings destroyed, its original dignity is still evident. The mansion with its gardens occupied the full northern half of the block bounded by Fairfax, Cameron, Lee and King Streets. On the East the property fell away rapidly to the river allowing a magnificent view of the Potomac from the rear terrace. Both plan and setting were originally very similar to that of nearby Mount Vernon. No doubt Carlyle House and Mount Airy of similar design were great influences in young Washington's decision to follow this formal plan when ordering the creative changes at Mount Vernon, carried out in 1758. Clearly a country house, it is unique in Alexandria, though nearby Annapolis still boasts three examples of this general architectural form, of slightly later date—circa 1765-70. Yet none of these had fully paneled rooms, while the Carlyle House, as well as Mount Airy and Mount Vernon, all contained splendid examples of this superlative wall treatment.

The "undertakers" or architect builders of the Eighteenth Century and their clients used the magnificent English folios of architectural engravings to an extent which is frequently not realized. Practically every important structure erected in this country from 1700 to 1830

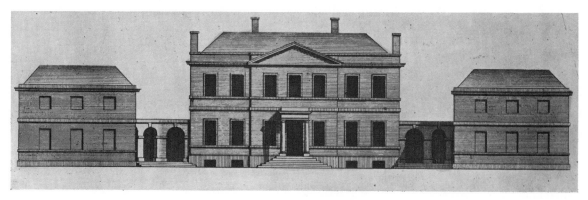

Another plate in the Gibbs' folio of 1728

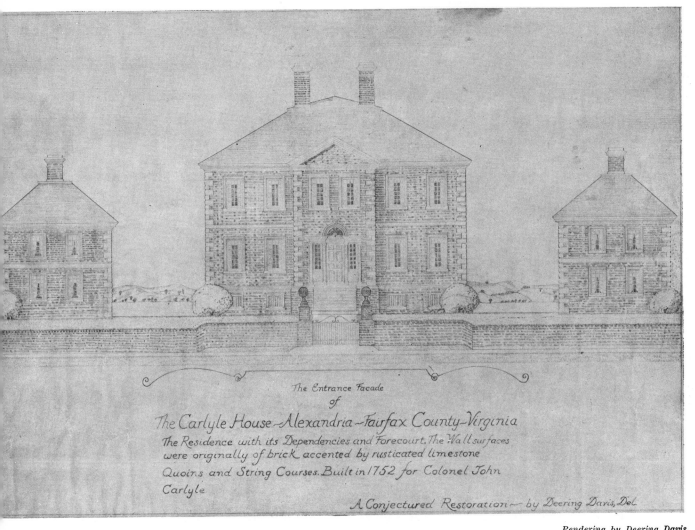

The Entrance Facade
of
The Carlyle House—Alexandria—Fairfax County—Virginia
The Residence with its Dependencies and Forecourt. The Wall surfaces
were originally of brick accented by rusticated limestone
Quoins and String Courses. Built in 1752 for Colonel John
Carlyle

A Conjectured Restoration—by Deering Davis, Del.

The Carlyle House

123 North Fairfax Street

is directly traceable to these sources—either as a direct copy or, as is more frequently the case, as a combination of modifications and simplifications to the point of becoming a new design. As these volumes were expensive and rare, the few available in a particular community had much to do with the creation of "local idiom." Many theories are advanced for the persistence of a particular style of design in a given locale, such as that of the mid-Georgian in Alexandria, but the obvious conclusion that the later folios were not locally obtainable is usually missed. It is frequently not realized that Hoban's winning design for the White House in 1792 without doubt has its prototype in the Folio by James Gibbs printed in London in 1728—thus directly carrying over a Georgian style into the Federal Period. Interior details of mantels, overmantels, doors and paneling were even more dependent on these volumes than were the actual structures.

"Vitruvius Scoticus" is such a folio of Scottish buildings designed by William Adam, architect father of Robert Adam who, with his two brothers was the creator of the almost universally known style which bears their name. This volume and that by Gibbs is known to have been available to Alexandrians in 1750. Craigie Hall (top page 50) designed by William Adam for Charles Hope, ancestor of Lord Roseberry, appears in it, and this design combined with some details from Gibbs (bottom page 50) was undoubtedly the source of inspiration to the creator of Carlyle House. Moreover there is no mere copying here, and the simplified and rescaled result is more pleasing than its more ornate prototypes.

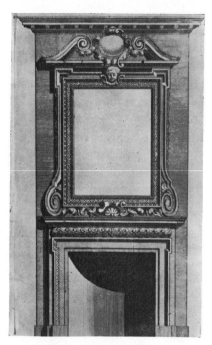

A chimney-piece from the Gibbs' folio 1728

In 1820 the Carlyle House was remodeled in the Federal manner. Entrance door, stairway, window trim and most of the mantels were changed. Later even more severe modifications were undertaken. The river facade may be seen from the warehouse district below it, though so altered by a Victorian veranda that its beauty is as effectively masked as it is from the West.

All the more surprising is the fact that the historic Blue Room and the small adjoining library remain much as General Braddock knew them in 1755. The original paneled doors have unfortunately been replaced, but their loss constitutes the only change of any importance. At one time Henry Ford attempted to buy the mansion and move it to his famous transplanted Colonial Village at Dearborn, Michigan. Happily nothing came of the negotiation, and it is now owned by Lloyd Diehl Schaeffer who operates it as a museum. It is hoped that in the not too distant future it may be handsomely and completely restored along with the rest of the block on which it stands and with that containing Gadsby's Tavern. Certainly its architectural excellence as one of the finest of America's mid-Eighteenth Century mansions, its rich history and its proximity to the National Capital warrant such a step.

The Carlyle House—Blue Room

Meeting place of the Colonial Governors in 1755; the room is noteworthy for its bold scrolled pediments above the doors and the superb chimney-piece with marble fireplace facing framed in egg-and-dart moulding. The overmantel was probably intended to support a similar pediment omitted for lack of space. The chair rail carries a Greek Key fret, and the cornice is enriched with carved rosettes between the modillions.

Mount Ver

West Entrance Facade

West Elevation of Mount Vernon showing the Origional Design as completed for George Washington in 1758.

Mount Vernon as completed in 1759 pursuant to the instructions of George Washington. As there were no major changes from 1759 to 1774 the period which encompassed all but

The Siding of the Main House is of Wood beveled
and sand dashed to simulate rusticated stone.
The Dependencies are also of Wood.

Conjectured Restoration by Deering Davis, Del.

the last two years in which the first President lived on his Plantation, it was this house and not the mansion we see today which was actually the home of America's foremost citizen.

MOUNT VERNON

SO MUCH HAS BEEN WRITTEN about Mount Vernon that it is difficult to approach the subject again without some trepidation. However, no architectural account of Alexandria should pass over the most important structure in its environs, the country seat of its first citizen. Therefore the portion of this volume devoted to pre-Revolutionary domestic structures could not be concluded without photographs of and comments on Mount Vernon, one of the most beautiful and surely the best known private residence in this country.

There is recently disclosed evidence, both historical and archaeological, that there was a dwelling on the Mount Vernon site as early as the last decade of the Seventeenth Century. The structure which General Washington remodelled and enlarged into the Mansion we know is believed to have had its origin in the cottage constructed by his father, Augustine, on the foundations of the earlier family homestead. Augustine Washington moved his family from the plantation in Westmoreland County (later Wakefield) to "Hunting Creek" Plantation on the upper reaches of the Potomac (later Mount Vernon) in 1735, when George was an infant of three years. There they resided until 1739, when he removed them to "Ferry Farm" or "Pine Grove" as it was also called opposite Fredericksburg, where he died in 1743 and where Mary Ball Washington, his widow, passed most of her life.

In 1740 Augustine Washington deeded the property to his eldest son, Lawrence, half-brother of George, and the gift was later confirmed by will. In 1743, with his bride, Anne Fairfax of Belvoir, Lawrence Washington came to settle upon his estate, which he named "Mount Vernon" after his former commanding officer in the West Indies, Admiral Vernon of the Royal Navy.

Lawrence Washington died at the age of thirty-four in 1752, bequeathing Mount Vernon to his infant daughter Sarah. On her death in 1754 George Washington, who had lived with his brother since he was sixteen, inherited the estate of 2500 acres.

In 1758 after five years of intermittent Indian fighting and frontier exploration he became engaged to Martha Dandridge Custis of New Kent County, the richest widow in the Colonies. He was only twenty-six, and quite naturally wishing to impress his bride, he planned, and had quickly executed, such major changes in the house that this date becomes the architectural birthday of Mount Vernon as we know it today.

The interior illustrations given here show the house in this, its principal design phase. Few realize that the present Mansion, incorporating the additions completed in 1787, was occupied by our First President for less than three years.

The House which was home to George Washington and his family for the 15 years (1759-74) and in which he established himself as a leading agriculturist and power in the community was smaller and simpler, such as any successful man of that day or this could well afford. The enlarged version familiar to most of us was necessitated later by the great number of visitors attracted by the owner's fame, position and wealth.

The Augustine-Lawrence Washington house of one and one-half stories had contained four rooms on the ground floor connected by a central hall, while the second story had four bed chambers plus a small hall room. By 1759 the roof had been raised to make a full two-story and attic building, with single chimneys at each end. The exterior walls were unusually finished in beveled boards painted white and sanded to simulate cut stone as at Mount Airy and two small identical out-buildings were erected near the west corners of the edifice, deviating from the usual formal mid-Georgian-plan of most of the other Virginia Country Seats in that they were placed at an angle with the Great House. There were no connecting arcades in this 1760 version, but the buildings were joined by brick walls surmounted by what Washington called a "Pallisade" (probably a picket fence). This design gave the appearance of a curved plan and added to its overall length. Most of the great houses of America built before 1765 did not have connections with their dependencies. Probably fear of fire starting in the kitchen was the cause of their omission.

Photograph: Frances Benjamin Johnston, courtesy Mount Vernon Ladies Association

The stair ordered in 1758. The balusters were made by Lamphere, the joyner in Alexandria. The fine paneling and overdoor pediments were installed at the same time. Today their original lovely soft grey-green paint has been carefully restored.

For reasons of family sentiment, desire for haste, or economy, the original corner chimneys were retained, giving a very early architectural character to the rooms and making it difficult to place furniture in a symmetrical manner. These fireplaces and the slightly off-center entrance must have caused the General many moments of annoyance due to his profound admiration of classic balance. The irregular placement of the west facade door was caused by the new main stairs which were installed in 1758. The balustrade now leading to the attic is in all probability the original one from the earlier house.

After 1773 there were numerous alterations but these were expansions rather than changes in the original design. Even the famous East Portico is an enlargement of the 1758 version. New service dependencies were added nearby—there were eventually twenty-odd—and Washington made plans calling for the extension of the main mass to provide for a banquet hall on the north and a library on the south ends as at present. By the time of the General's departure in 1775 the library was under construction. Throughout his absence during the war the remodeling continued according to detailed instructions written to his overseer, Lund Washington. Thus the banquet hall was begun in 1778 and the curved passageways completed. Even these last alterations ordered by Washington, with the exception of the interior decorative details of the banquet hall, were conceived, though not executed, before the Revolution and are thoroughly mid-Georgian in character. The interior of the banquet hall alone is in the Adam version of the succeeding Federal style.

The plantation itself was expanded until it included eight thousand acres. During his years of absence as General and as President he planned for the days when he might return to the peaceful life of the country squire and the enjoyment of his estate. He was given that enjoyment for only two years and nine months after his final return to Mount Vernon where he died on December 14, 1799 at sixty-seven.

There is much speculation in certain circles as to whether or not George Washington was the architect of Mount Vernon. Of course the definition of the word architect must first be agreed upon. Its present legal definition as a person with a state license to practice the profession of architecture is only about 30 years old and one may still practice in two states in this country without a license. Chippendale referred to himself as an architect. One should use the term meaning "the designer of an edifice" when speaking of old buildings. After much research and several complete reversals of opinion we now firmly believe that Washington's own ideas were the real design factor in the planning of Mount Vernon. Certainly no master builder such as Buckland or Ariss would have so placed the stairs as to force the entrance off center, nor would he have retained the small rooms and old-fashioned awkward corner fireplaces. These seem to be the decisions of a young amateur. Ten years later, we doubt that they would have been made. Though as a younger son he was given a practical education as a surveyor instead of the dilletante architectural training fashionable at that time for young aristocrats, his greater than ordinary interest in such matters, plus his intimacy with the Fairfaxes, would have more than made up for this deficiency. His mentor, Thomas Lord Fairfax, was a gentleman of culture and enormous wealth. Surely his library contained an unusual number of English architectural folios for the young surveyor to pore over and educate his taste. Existing drawings show him to have been a competent draftsman. His letters constantly indicate his great interest in architecture. Though he professed ignorance more than once, we believe this to be a polite habit of the time, not to be taken too literally. We know he often sought advice but that is only the intelligent thing to do. His very keenness of interest made him susceptible to what he saw and admired, hence we believe that Gadsby's, the Carlyle House, and Mount Airy had much to do with the design of Mount Vernon. Furniture, paintings, and sculpture were also given much detailed attention. Washington was very aware of the latest fashion. His appreciation of French furnishings set the mode in the Executive Mansions in both New York and Philadelphia. Upon his retirement from the Presidency, many pieces in the Louis XVI manner were sent on to Mount Vernon and in recent years a number of them have been returned to their accus-

Photograph: Rex Curtiss of Harris & Ewing

A perfect example of George Washington's interest in and attention to artistic details. A letter of 1757 to his London agents ordering this landscape still exists. The charm and "finished" appearance gained by the picture exactly fitting the overmantel frame is very apparent. The difficulties in obtaining paintings of proper size caused this design rule to be widely neglected in the Colonies.

tomed place through the efforts of the Mount Vernon Ladies' Association. Of particular note are the shaving stand and lady's writing desk, which were purchased by Washington in 1789 from the Comte de Moustiers, retiring French Ambassador. These pieces, together with a typical Louis XVI bergère and a stool, are exhibited in the bedroom where he died. Our first president's stamp of approval on the French taste has undoubtedly had a great, if unobtrusive, influence on American styles.

As early as 1757 General Washington had shown a predilection for decorative plaster work by ordering gesso ornaments from England to be applied to the West Parlor ceilings.

At the beginning of the Revolutionary War, he sought to improve on these decorations by having a French artisan redecorate the ceiling and chimney piece of the dining room at Mount Vernon. The same workman had decorated the walls of Betty Washington Lewis' (his sister) place, "Mill Brook" (later Kenmore) in Fredericksburg and a number of the motifs are the same. The work was so consuming of time that the General evidently expressed a fear that the plaster must be over-elaborate. Reassuring him, Lund Washington wrote on November 12, 1775: "The stucco man agrees the ceiling is a handsomer one than any of Col. Lewis's, although not half the work on it." He then added: "It was a plan recommended by Sears." As completed, the ceiling was so similar to a design appearing in an eighteenth century English architectural book by William Pain, that one must conclude that work was familiar to either or both of the craftsmen; unimpeachible evidence of the influence on design which the artisan and his Folio of English Plates exercised. It is a matter of interest that the ornament is entirely characteristic of the earlier style of Louis XV.

Due to the increasing efforts of the Mount Vernon Ladies' Association much of the original furniture after being widely scattered for over 100 years has returned. Very recently an unusual number of original items have been acquired. The Mount Vernon Ladies' Association is tireless in its efforts to restore the house exactly as our first president knew and loved it. The amount of research which has been done and the wealth of material discovered could fill many large and interesting volumes yet the work continues with ever-renewed enthusiasm.

MOUNT VERNON WALL-PAPERS

by Nancy McClelland, A.I.D.

Judging from the frequent references to wall-paper found in Washington's correspondence with his purchasing agents and with the managers of Mount Vernon, it looks as though the General from the first intended to paper most of the rooms in the Mansion. He loved wall-paper!

As early as November 1757, three years after inheriting the estate, he received from England a sizable shipment of wall-papers, which are described in an invoice that has been carefully preserved. There was "blue embost paper" for one room, and "green embost paper" for another; "yellow embost paper" for a third, as well as "India figured paper," "chintz paper" and "crimson embost paper" for three other rooms.

These papers may have been used in preparing Mount Vernon for the reception of his bride, Martha Custis, and perhaps they gave the names to certain bedrooms in Mount Vernon, which have always been known as the "Blue Room," the "Green Room" and the "Yellow Room."

At a later date, in 1794, Washington instructed William Pearce in a letter:

"When you next go to Alexandria take the exact dimensions of the rooms in my house at that place, that I may send paper for them. Give the length and breadth of each, and height from the wash-board to the chair-board (as they are commonly called) and thence to the cornish, if any, with the doors and windows, and the size of them, in each room or passage. If there is occasion to make good the plastering in any of the rooms, no white-

Photograph: Rex Curtiss of Harris & Ewing

This lovely simple mantel is very like those in Gadsby's Tavern. Probably Lamphere was the craftsman in both instances. The Gaming Table and simple early Chippendale Chair were Washington pieces. The hand tufted rug has the date 1748 woven in the border.

The study mantel planned in 1774. Both the chimney-piece and the panels are essentially Mid-Georgian Design but the later classic style ornamental details make the former a Transition type.

The Dining Room Mantel, circa 1775

An example of Louis XV influence on English design showing asymmetrically balanced Rocaille plaster ornamentation. It is the handicraft of the artisan who did similar work at Kenmore, and to whom Washington referred as the "Frenchman." Documents show that Sears the joyner in Alexandria made the wooden portion of this piece in 1775.

wash is to be put thereon, because it is improper for paper. . . . It is not usual, nor is there any occasion for Papering the ceiling of the Room or rooms (if more than one of the Room, or rooms, should be papered) in the House in Alexandria."

Such detailed instructions and remarks of the original owner were of great assistance when in 1940 the Mount Vernon Ladies' Association of which Mrs. Towner was then Regent, and the Mansion Committee with Mrs. Benjamin Warren at its head, decided to refurbish and restore the bedrooms of Mount Vernon. Mr. Herbert A. Claiborne of Richmond, an architect specializing in 18th Century restorations, worked with the committee, and I was called into consultation about the wall-papers.

I still remember with the keenest delight the time we spent in studying the various rooms. With great care, Mr. Claiborne scraped away layers of paint from a bit of woodwork, until the bottom layer had been reached and the original color was apparent. In the room used as a bedroom by General and Mrs. Washington before the house was enlarged to Mansion proportions, we found that the original paint was a lovely old green color. But the room was known as the "Yellow Room," so the paper must have been largely yellow in tone. This decided us to use on the walls a careful reproduction of an old paper which bore the stamp tax of George III. With a background of yellow and designs in gray and green it harmonized delightfully with the green woodwork.

We also found in Washington's diary of September 7, 1786, the following entry about this room: "Began to paper the Yellow Room this day—Majr Washington and Thos Green the undertakers—On the directions I received *with the paper from England.*" All of which helped to confirm our selection.

The little hall-bedroom, which was used by George Washington Parke Custis, Nelly's brother and the builder of "Arlington House," called for a wall-paper of small design. We used a French hand-blocked paper in a Pillement design and finished it with a wall-paper border all around the top of the room. There are many references in Washington's letter to this use of borders. In one epistle he writes to Clement Biddle of Philadelphia: "I shall be obliged to you for sending me seventy yards of gilded border for papered Rooms (of the kind you shewed me when I was in Philadelphia). That which is most light and airy I should prefer. I do not know whether it is usual to fasten it on with brads or Glew—if the former, I must beg that as many be sent as will answer this purpose."

In the Nellie Custis Room we used large sheets of a French paper which was partly hand-blocked and partly colored by hand with a brush. This was known as the "Carnation paper." Mrs. Towner described it as "having exactly the same feeling as the rug in this room."

All of these papers, as well as the "Cenelle" paper in the Lafayette room are authentic reproductions of Eighteenth Century papers to the last detail, and, like all early wall-papers, are printed by hand on pure linen paper.

When it came to the "Blue Bedroom," which was used as a guest room in the days of Washington, a paper was suggested which had been reproduced from an old fragment hung behind a door in Glebe House, Woodbury, Connecticut. Miss Annie Jennings, a board member of Glebe House, (which is owned by the Episcopal Church) was long a Vice-Regent of Mount Vernon; with Bishop Budlong's permission the paper was especially printed for use in this Mount Vernon guest room. The reproduction rights are the property of the Mount Vernon Ladies' Association.

Meticulous care was used in every room to have only Eighteenth Century designs, of the early period of the house.

The paper now in the room where Washington died must have been installed in the house at a much later date, since the design is around 1820 or 1830. It was discovered in 1931 by Mr. Dodge, the former superintendent, under a layer of plaster at the right of the fireplace in the room, but probably was never seen by the first President of the United States.

The paper in the entrance hall is also a reproduction of later-than-Eighteenth-Century date.

Photograph: Rex Curtiss of Harris & Ewing

The bedroom of General and Mrs. Washington for the fifteen years prior to the 1774 addition. The unusual chair has Queen Ann legs and seat while the pierced splat and square corners of the back show a Chippendale trend. The wall paper in this room is an exact reproduction of an English paper which bore the Tax Stamp of George III. Printed in yellow, gray and green, it harmonizes with the old green color of the woodwork, which was discovered by scraping off various layers until the original coat of paint came to light.

GEORGE WASHINGTON'S TOWN HOUSE

A CHAPTER DEVOTED to Mount Vernon and other Washington holdings, which is included in a volume on Alexandria's Architecture, should not close without at least a brief account of the family's properties in the town itself. At the first auction sale of lots, July 13, 1749, Lawrence Washington, George's elder half-brother and the proprietor of Mount Vernon, purchased number 51 for 31 Pistoles and number 52 for 16 Pistoles, sums which clearly indicate that these lots on the South side of King Street between Water (now Lee) and Fairfax were among the most desirable to be had. No. 51 was on the waterfront, while number 52, an ideal home site, topped a steep bank overlooking the harbor, the broad Potomac, and the lovely Maryland shore. A dwelling appears to have been built in compliance with the regulations for "improving" property, as George Washington in his diary of 1760 refers to his house in Alexandria. It is probable that he referred to Lawrence Washington's as "his" since he was the executor of that estate. Today warehouses and mercantile shops occupy this block.

Augustine, Lawrence's younger full brother, bought lots 64 and 65 for 15 Pistoles on July 14, 1749. June 18, 1754 this property on the South side of Prince between Lee and Fairfax was ordered resold by the Trustees of the town as the regulation stipulating that they must be "improved" (built upon) had not been met. William Ramsay purchased them on September 9, 1754 for 37 pounds, 1 shilling, 9 pence showing a considerable increase in real estate values during the five year interval.

At the auction held May 9, 1763 which established the town's first addition, George Washington bought lot 112 on the northwest corner of Prince and Pitt Streets for 38 pounds and lot 118 on the southwest corner of Cameron and Pitt for ten pounds ten shillings. Documentary evidence shows us that 112 was unimproved until 1790 when it was sub-divided into nine lots to be built upon and let at annual ground rent. At least one house was completed here before the General's death in 1799.

Our first President had ordered built for his personal convenience, as early as 1765, a very simple dwelling, a stable and other necessary buildings on lot 118. This place was often rented or lent to members of the family and friends; Dr. Brown lived there for some time. One of Washington's letters refers to spending the night "at my own house." Others order fencing for the property, give detailed directions for repairing the fireplaces, laying a brick floor in the basement, papering the bedroom wall, painting the exterior stone color, etc. At her death Mrs. Washington left this property to her nephew Bartholomew Dandridge. The original half acre purchase bounded by the corner of Pitt and Cameron Streets is now divided into seven lots.

Unfortunately the dwelling was destroyed in 1854, and its site is now a garden. The only pictorial representation of it which so far has been discovered is a crude drawing made just after the structure's demolition by a Miss Mary Stewart who had always lived across the street and therefore quite probably gave a generally accurate picture. Mr. Worth Bailey on the staff at Mount Vernon feels that the Restoration Drawing (page 69) based on Miss Stewart's sketch supplemented by her written description, plus the numerous references in the writings of General Washington, gives an accurate picture of his Alexandria house. It, along with the town square, should be carefully restored.

c.1765
George Washington's Town House
Alexandria, Virginia
A Conjectured Restoration

by Deering Davis, Del.

CHRIST CHURCH, circa 1773

Southwest Corner of Cameron and Columbus Streets

In Christ Church a silver plate marks the Washington pew which he purchased for the sum of thirty-six pounds, ten shillings. In this same pew Prime Minister Churchill worshipped with the late President Roosevelt on a memorable Sunday in January 1942 when the horror of Pearl Harbor was still fresh. In this church, too, the beloved General Robert E. Lee was confirmed. His pew likewise is marked by a silver plate.

The acre of land on which this building of the Established Church of Virginia was erected was given by John Alexander of Stafford. In 1767 James Parsons agreed to build the church for £600, but the contract was not fulfilled and it was finished for an additional £220 by John Carlyle in 1773. In the same year James Wren received £8 to "Write the Lord's Prayer, the Creed and the Ten Commandments" on panels which may be seen today on each side of the pulpit. In 1785 the galleries were added, in 1810 an organ was installed and the tower and steeple erected and the bell hung in 1818.

George Washington was one of the twelve vestrymen chosen by the Parish in 1765. He remained a communicant and contributor until his death when his funeral service was conducted at Mount Vernon by the Reverend Thomas Davis, the rector. His Bible was presented to the church by the General's adopted son, George Washington Parke Custis in 1804. Among Christ Church's early rectors was the Reverend Bryan Fairfax of Mount Eagle who later became 8th Baron Fairfax of Cameron and who was a brother of Sara (Fairfax) Carlyle.

During the Civil War and the Federal occupation when Army chaplains served the pul-

View from the Churchyard showing part of the steeple erected in 1818

pit and Northerners were installed as vestrymen, the majority of the parish left to hold their services elsewhere—not to return until after the Federal soldiers left. In the churchyard with its great trees may be seen the tomb of the Confederate soldiers who died in the city's hospitals during the war and many monuments to those connected with Alexandria's founding.

71

The Old Presbyterian Meeting House, circa 1774 (restored)

321 South Fairfax Street

While the dislike of the Scots for ostentation is well illustrated in the functional simplicity of this old church finished in 1774, the delicate and unusual long iron rail at the entrance is very fine.   Partially destroyed by fire in 1835, the church was rebuilt the following year.   Around it are the graves of such prominent early citizens as John Carlyle, Dennis Ramsay and Dr. James Craik.

The Dr. Brown House, circa 1775

212 South Fairfax Street

Dr. Brown, a physician, who attended George Washington, lived in this house

THE CRAIK HOUSE
Circa 1775
210 Duke Street

This house known for its fine interior finish was built about 1775 by George Coryell for Dr. James Craik who had been born at Dumfries, Scotland, in 1730 and had practiced medicine both in the West Indies and Winchester, Virginia, before coming to Alexandria. In 1754 he was commissioned as Surgeon in Colonel Fry's Regiment over which Washington assumed command when Fry died. Thus began the long and intimate friendship between these men which ended only when on Saturday December 15, 1799, Craik, as he wrote "kissed the cold hand which I held in my bosom, laid it down, and for some time was lost in profound grief." To him the General bequeathed his desk and chair, now returned to their place in the library of Mt. Vernon.

The doctor had been appointed Assistant Director General of Hospitals for the Continental Army and according to Mary L. Powell, "from the field of Great Meadows until Yorktown he was with Washington in every battle. He ministered to the dying Braddock, saw Hugh Mercer breathe his last at Princeton, and young George Johnston die at Morristown, New Jersey, dressed Lafayette's wounds at Brandywine, and stood with Washington at the death bed of John Parke Custis, just after the surrender of the British at Yorktown."

The Craik's were popular socially in the city and the doctor's practice was extensive. He maintained it until old age compelled him to retire to his country estate, "Vaucleuse." He died there in 1814 at the age of eighty-four and was buried in the old Presbyterian meetinghouse yard. He was the father of nine children, and one of his sons, who later became Postmaster of Alexandria in 1807-8, served as private secretary to Washington during two years of the Revolution.

Photograph: Harris & Ewing

The present owners Dr. and Mrs. Laurence Thompson have beautifully restored this charming house. The brick addition to the left is in reality an old wood siding "flounder" house which has been faced with brick and joined to the main house.

219 North Royal Street

This house, built on an original lot of 1749, and now owned by Mr. and Mrs. Mangum Weeks, well illustrates the pre-Revolutionary masonry. The brickwork and Aquia Creek sandstone steps have acquired the patina of time. Characteristic are the long "flounder" ell, walled garden, coach-yard and Eighteenth Century brick coach-house, one of few now left.

76

Photograph: Mangum Weeks

219 North Royal Street

This charming chimneypiece shows the final Colonial phase of fireplace mantling, in which a full architectural order replaces the simple architrave. Three contemporary portraits of eminent related Virginians hang above: General Washington's family, Colonel Parke of Blenheim fame, and General Lee.

200 Prince Street

The Second Floor Parlor

This fine room, circa 1780, was removed from the large hiproofed house at the corner of Prince and South Lee Streets, and now appropriately furnished as of the period, is in the City Art Museum, St. Louis, Mo.

Another view of the same room

The Dulaney House, circa 1785
601 Duke Street

This is now the residence of Mr. and Mrs. John Howard Joynt who have, as the following photographs show, furnished it beautifully and correctly. LaFayette stayed here on two separate occasions. The Dulaneys were famous for their hospitality, both here at their "Town House" as well as at their country estate.

Photograph : Peggy Duffy

The Living Room door with fine original brass lock

Photograph: Peggy Duffy

The Second Parlor—superb antique furniture in keeping with this distinguished room

Photograph: Peggy Duffy

Interior architecture and furniture of distinction

Photograph: Woltz

The Dining Room, located in an ell of later date, lacks the distinguished wood trim of the earlier part, but the superb Queen Ann furniture and wall paper atone for its absence.

The stair and entrance hall

Photograph: Peggy Duffy

Fine woodwork of the Pre-Revolutionary type prevails throughout the major portion of the house. An excellent example of the "hold over" style in Alexandria.

Another bedroom mantel showing adherence to the earlier design

ROBERT E. LEE HOUSE
607 Oronoco Street

One of a pair, the Lee House was begun in about 1793 and completed in 1795 by John Potts who sold it in 1799 to Colonel William Fitzhugh of "Chatham" near Fredericksburg. Shortly before his death, Washington dined as a guest for the last time on November 17, 1799 in this house. He had come to Alexandria to church and stopped for dinner with his life-long friend, Colonel Fitzhugh, before beginning the return trip to "Mount Vernon."

Fitzhugh's only daughter, Mary Lee, married George Washington Parke Custis on July 7, 1804, and left this house to become the mistress of "Arlington," north of the town on the hills above the Potomac. After the death of her husband, Mrs. Henry Lee, moved to this house, bringing her son Robert E. Lee, then eleven years old. The future general, after receiving his primary education at Alexandria Academy, was prepared for West Point at the Hallowell School next door. During these years he was a frequent visitor at "Arlington," and two years after his graduation from the Military Academy he married Mary, the only child of George Washington Parke Custis, and as a result later became the master of Arlington.

The Quaker schoolmaster, Benjamin Hallowell, who conducted an excellent school in the house at 609 Oronoco Street, speaks in his journal under date of October 17, 1825 of standing at the doorstep with his bride of one day to see General Lafayette pass on his way to call on the widow of General Henry Lee next door. Before Hallowell's occupancy, this house was the residence of William Hodgeson, an Englishman who had married the daughter of William Lee, one of the first American envoys abroad during the Revolution.

Both houses are distinctive for their widely spaced windows, dentiled cornices and long gabled roofs with only two dormers, each separated by small classic pediments which are pierced by oval lights. The slightly projecting central portions of the facades topped by the pediments carry the entrance doors. Windows are accented by keystones and lintels of white stone. The scale is delicate and while it preserves certain mid-Georgian features, it shows a marked sympathy for the Federal style.

The Hallowell School and the Robert E. Lee House, circa 1800

609-607 Oronoco Streets

The famous old school appears prominently while only the entrance door of its twin, the Lee House, is visible at the far right of the photograph.

THE GENERAL HENRY LEE HOUSE
Circa 1800
611 Cameron Street

Henry Lee, soldier, statesman, orator, historian—distinguished father of a distinguished son, moved to this house in 1811 from "Stratford," his estate in Westmoreland County in order to see to the primary education of his three sons in Alexandria.

Born in 1756, he was at Princeton when the Revolution broke out, and entering the Army at nineteen, fought throughout the war. His leadership, courage and initiative during the campaigns in New York, Pennsylvania and New Jersey marked him as an outstanding officer, and as Major in command of the cavalry unit known as "Lee's Legion"—many of whose members were Alexandria men—he served most successfully in South Carolina under General Greene. In 1794 while Governor of Virginia he commanded the militia sent to Pennsylvania to crush the Whiskey Rebellion, and in 1799 as a member of Congress delivered the eulogy on Washington containing the famous phrase "First in war, first in peace, first in the hearts of his countrymen." After the death of his first wife he married Ann Hill Carter of "Shirley." To them were born Charles Carter, Sidney Smith and Robert Edward Lee.

When the war of 1812 appeared imminent, Congress offered him a commission as Major General, but on the way to join his command he received a wound from which he never recovered, in an encounter with a Baltimore mob. He spent several years in the West Indies in an unsuccessful effort to regain his health, and on his way home, died on the Georgia plantation of his old friend, General Nathaniel Greene in March 1818. Almost one hundred years later the bones of brave, able, reckless "Light Horse Harry" were brought back to Virginia where they rest near those of his great and revered son in the crypt at Lexington.

The house like its architectural counterpart next door, is of simple, two story and dormered attic type. A transition example of particular interest is the wider doorway with side lights which is more characteristic of the Federal than the mid-Georgian style.

Photograph: Harris & Ewing

Major General Henry Lee, father of Robert E. Lee, moved to this house from his estate "Stratford" in 1811.   He served as Governor of Virginia, and as a Member of Congress.

THE LLOYD HOUSE
Circa 1800

220 North Washington Street

This large house built in 1793 by James Hooe is one of the most pleasing examples of Georgian domestic architecture in a city rich in that idiom of design. It was used by Benjamin Hallowell for several years to house his school, and on the death of Mr. Hooe's widow was sold at public auction in 1832, to John Lloyd, in whose family possession of it remained for almost one hundred years.

In this house Robert E. Lee learned of his appointment by the Virginia State Legislature to command the Army of Virginia. When he stopped at the Lloyd's on his way home to "Arlington" from Christ Church the day after he had resigned his commission as Colonel in the United States Army, Colonel Lee received the first news of the legislature's decision to tender command of its new army to him.

Dating as it does from 1793 the house is an example of the holdover style in Alexandria. The only Federal detail is to be found in the interior trim which is of modified Adam type. The exterior however is decidedly in the mid-Georgian vein so popular in Alexandria. The structure is of rectangular plan of dark red brick in Flemish bond. The dentiled cornice continues around the building framing the gable ends. The chimney tops are slightly moulded and the corners which relieve the roof surfaces carry the same pediment resting on pilasters, as that surmounting the door. The pedimented doorway itself is one of the best among the fine ones that epitomize Alexandria building, and the brick of the facade is relieved by lintels and keystones of white stone.

The Lloyd House

The beautiful doorway is a typical product of Alexandria craftsmanship of the late Eighteenth Century. The unusual entices supporting the pilasters are worthy of note.

Window detail—note the fine moulded sill and fluted key-block

103 to 113 Prince Street

This charming row of small early nineteenth century houses on Prince Street has been carefully restored. Several of them once housed ship captains whose sailing craft took Virginia products to far places and brought

back many of the heirlooms that furnish Alexandria houses. Bordered
with the green of poplars and the rose and white of its old dwellings, this
rough cobbled block of Prince Street, leading down to the warehouses and
the quiet waters of the Potomac at its foot, makes time retrace its steps to
another century.

The Leadbeater House, circa 1800

329 North Washington Street

The third story was added about 1830

98

105-107 South Fairfax Street

In this building Stabler Leadbeater established an apothecary's shop in 1792. The bow windows are reminiscent of early shops in old London.

609-611 Queen Street, circa 1800

Photograph: Harris & Ewing

215 Jefferson Street, circa 1800

Built as a home for one of the sons of the founder of Alexandria, this house has a facade of good proportions. The stone arch and impost blocks at the entrance are not typical of houses of the period in Alexandria.

THE LORD FAIRFAX HOUSE
Circa 1816

607 Cameron Street

Thomas Lord Fairfax, 9th Baron Cameron, and head of that great Virginia family, used this house as a winter residence until his death in 1846. It then passed to his son, Dr. Orlando Fairfax, a prominent physician of Alexandria, in whose ownership it remained until after the Civil War. The house was built in 1816 on land leased from Charles Alexander by William Yeaton who came to Alexandria in 1800. The first great Virginia landowner of the family, an earlier Baron Cameron, whose lands comprised one-fifth of the present State of Virginia, offered George Washington a post as a surveyor to assist in laying out his great manor of "Greenaway Court" near the Blue Ridge. The title passed first to a younger brother and then to the Reverend Bryan Fairfax, the son of Colonel William Fairfax of "Belvoir."

During the Revolution the Fairfaxes remained loyal to the mother country. Bryan Fairfax attempted to dissuade Washington from taking any part against the Crown, and although he was completely unsuccessful, they remained neighbors and close friends. He was ordained by Bishop Seabury in 1790 and for two years was rector of Christ Church, Alexandria. He succeeded to the title in 1800 and died at "Mount Eagle," his estate, two miles southwest of Alexandria in 1802. His son, Thomas, who succeeded him, inherited over forty thousand acres in Fairfax County where he lived as a country squire supervising the administration of his estates.

The residence which he purchased as a town house is of three-story rectangular plan with a two-story ell extending to the rear and a large garden at the side. The red brick facade is relieved by white stone string courses and lintels and by a single blind arch with stuccoed surface which contains the two center hall windows of the second and third stories. The entrance door is within an arched and deeply recessed vestibule and the interior is marked by particularly fine wood and composition trim of Adam inspiration.

Photograph: Harris & Ewing

This fine entrance with its curving steps and graceful railing is an outstanding example of early builders' work. Note the unusual muntin arrangement which forms a "transom" in the first story windows. The stone string-courses are of English antecedance.

Entrance Detail

The vestibule has curved ends and the arched ceiling follows the same curve, creating an unusual effect. Delicately carved woodwork adds to the charm of the builder's ingenuity.

A superb example of the Adam influence on the Federal style with elaborate applied gesso ornament.

The delicate gesso work and flat panels with applied mouldings constitute a pleasing detail.

The Spiral Stair of the Lord Fairfax House

303, 305, 307 North Washington Street, circa 1820

At this date small windows on the floor line were used instead of dormers

The LaFayette House, circa 1820

301 South St. Asapth Street

The balustrade is a later addition

Photograph: Harris & Ewing

819 and 817 Prince Street, circa 1800

The small Federal type at its best

THE SNOWDEN HOUSE
Circa 1790
611 South Lee Street

Known as the Snowden House after the family which occupied it for ninety-seven years of its long existence, this fine Georgian structure was built long before their ownership. It is not known which of the Alexanders built the house, but John Alexander gave the property to his son, William Thornton Alexander, who sold it to Thomas Vowell on August 29, 1798. It later came into the possession of the Snowdens.

The massive and dignified doorway is surmounted by a pediment, and the facade cornice is unusual and of fine workmanship. Although the original mantels have been replaced, the other details of the interior trim attest to the original elegance of the structure. The kitchen was once completely separated from the house and was later joined by a brick "bridge" between the two buildings, as illustrated on page 114. That the kitchens were very frequently separate outbuildings is indicated by the fact that often when this dependency was joined to the main house the ell fell directly behind the dining room or parlor, rather than to the rear of the hall—thus forcing a servant going from the rear of the house to pass through the dining room, or parlor, in order to reach the front door. The garden of the Snowden House is lovely and it once had an unusually fine view up and down the Potomac.

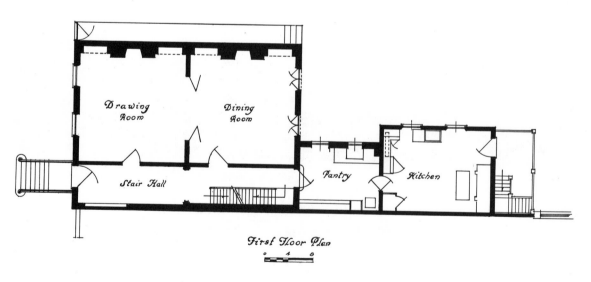

First Floor Plan

Typical first floor plan of the ell type house

112

Photograph: Library of Congress

Early builders paid much attention to fenestration and detail as is beautifully indicated in this residence of Justice and Mrs. Hugo Black.

The Garden Side

The ell, originally a separate dependency, has been rounded where it joins the main structure in order not to obstruct a window.

THE EDMUND JENNINGS LEE HOUSE, circa 1800

428 North Washington Street

Although built in 1799 this house is decidedly mid-Georgian in general feeling. Among the many houses in Alexandria occupied at one time or another by members of the Lee family, this is one of the more attractive architecturally. Built of brick in the form of a square plus an ell, it has an air of graceful solidity with its center chimney and dentiled cornice framing the gable ends as well as the front and rear eaves.

Edmund Jennings Lee, one of the four distinguished sons of Henry Lee of "Leesylvania," built the house. He argued and won the case for Christ Church, Alexandria, against the State of Virginia, which after the Revolution had confiscated for division among the poor all glebe lands originally allotted to the churches for their support. The vestry of Christ Church brought suit in 1802 and as a result of the decision declaring the confiscation unconstitutional regained its properties which were sold and the proceeds devoted to the building of a steeple and church yard wall and the purchase of a rectory and a bell.

Arch Hall, 815 Franklin Street, circa 1816

Arch Hall, built in 1816 has a plan which is singularly different from those of other early Alexandria houses. A one and a half story house having rooms of ample scale at each side of the central hall, it has, predominantly, an air of gracious hospitality. Second story bedrooms are lighted by windows in the gable ends. It was built as the town house of George Washington's nephew, and adopted granddaughter Mr. and **Mrs.** Lawrence Lewis, owners of beautiful Woodlawn adjoining the Mount Vernon estate.

Photograph: Harris & Ewing

The unusual entrance hall from which the house received its name

The Lyceum, circa 1837

201 South Washington Street

A very fine example of the beautiful American architectural style—Greek Revival

The stair is in its original condition, although the house was refurbished at a later date

IRON WORK

There is little or no Pre-Revolutionary iron work extant in Alexandria. This is especially disappointing because the hand forged pieces of this early period probably mark the zenith of the craft. However, there are numerous simple and very lovely examples of late Eighteenth Century design. Lightness of scale, simplicity and delicacy are their key notes, beautifully exemplified on the opposite page. Here the lyre motif so much used by our great furniture designer Duncan Phyfe is employed with charming effect. No finer prototype of the early Federal style could be desired.

Unfortunately, many of the fine old buildings have added heavy Victorian cast iron fences, hand rails, and balconies; or the common extruded type of wicket work. One glance shows their complete inappropriateness contrasted with the fine hand details of the houses themselves.

This fine railing at 323 South Fairfax Street is an excellent example of the early iron worker's art

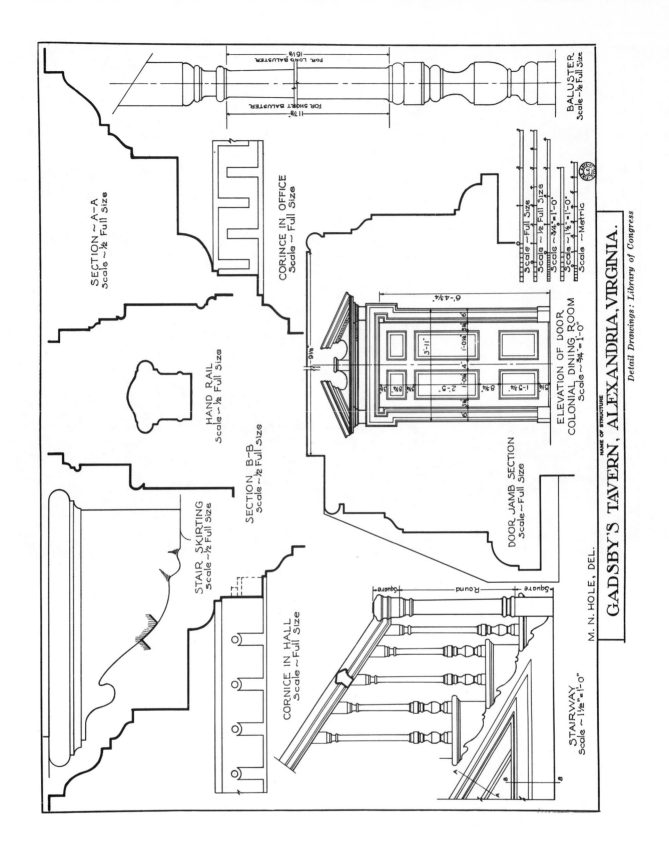

SECTION ~ A-A
Scale ~ ½ Full Size

CORNICE IN OFFICE
Scale ~ Full Size

BALUSTER
Scale ~ ½ Full Size

FOR LONG BALUSTER
16⅛"

FOR SHORT BALUSTER
11⅞"

HAND RAIL
Scale ~ ½ Full Size

SECTION ~ B-B
Scale ~ ½ Full Size

Scale ~ Full Size
Scale ~ ½ Full Size
Scale ~ ¾"=1'-0"
Scale ~ 1½"=1'-0"
Scale ~ Metric

ELEVATION OF DOOR
COLONIAL DINING ROOM
Scale ~ ¾"=1'-0"

6'-4¾"

3'-11"

1'-0½" 3½"

2'-5"

1'-5¾" 1'-0½"

4"

9½"

STAIR SKIRTING
Scale ~ ½ Full Size

DOOR JAMB SECTION
Scale ~ Full Size

CORNICE IN HALL
Scale ~ Full Size

Square
Round
Square

STAIRWAY
Scale ~ 1½"=1'-0"

M. N. HOLE, DEL.

NAME OF STRUCTURE

GADSBY'S TAVERN, ALEXANDRIA, VIRGINIA.

Detail Drawings : Library of Congress

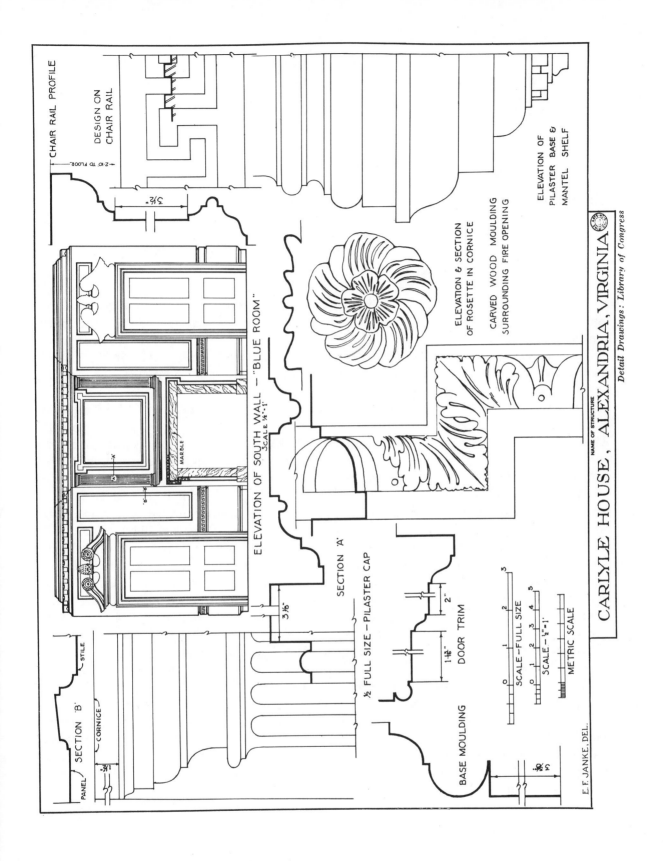

CHAIR RAIL PROFILE

DESIGN ON CHAIR RAIL

2'-10" TO FLOOR

3½"

ELEVATION OF PILASTER BASE & MANTEL SHELF

ELEVATION OF SOUTH WALL — "BLUE ROOM"
Scale ¼"=1'

MARBLE

ELEVATION & SECTION OF ROSETTE IN CORNICE

CARVED WOOD MOULDING SURROUNDING FIRE OPENING

SECTION 'A'

½ FULL SIZE — PILASTER CAP

2"

1⅜"

DOOR TRIM

3

SCALE — FULL SIZE

5

SCALE — ½"=1'

METRIC SCALE

BASE MOULDING

STILE

SECTION 'B'

CORNICE

PANEL

3½"

3/16"

E. F. JANKE, DEL.

NAME OF STRUCTURE

CARLYLE HOUSE, ALEXANDRIA, VIRGINIA

Detail Drawings : Library of Congress

ALEXANDRIA STRUCTURES
Erected Before 1830 and Still Extant

THE FOLLOWING LIST of structures erected in Alexandria before 1830 is submitted to show the volume of early American building still standing in the city and to offer a concise guide to those who wish to see its fine old houses.

It must be emphasized that while there has been a sincere effort to make it complete, in a project of this sort, there are inevitably unintentional omissions. The facades of many older houses were so altered during the Victorian era as to make their actual period unrecognizable to the passerby. Unless unlimited time is available, one making such a survey must depend to some extent upon the guidance and assistance of residents of the town under consideration. Without knowing it, he is almost certain to miss out-of-the-way examples in covering such a sizeable area with a very considerable grid of streets. Also in the case of small wooden structures of "tenement" type, alterations and replacements have been more easily made and often have concealed their true age.

At the same time it is equally certain that a few structures are included which may be as much as fifteen years younger than the authors believe them to be. As has been explained, Alexandria building is outstanding and almost unequaled in its devotion to transitional or "hold-over" styles. Alexandrians admired sound craftsmanship and in new buildings, particularly of the Georgian type, often retained those forms which time had already proven suitable to the local scene and pleasing to Alexandria eyes even when in nearby cities they had given way entirely to the newer mode. Similarly in estimating the age of an Alexandria dwelling and this must be done in most cases as records do not afford reliable data on building dates of the main structure on a particular city lot—one of Federal or Classic revival type which might with certainty be placed in the first two decades of the century elsewhere will prove on careful research to have been built in Alexandria a quarter century later. Finally, in recent years restoration or rebuilding of small wooden dwellings has been of such high caliber as to make the remodeled building appear considerably older than it actually is to one who cannot examine it with extreme care. (Weather boarding and trim is often replaced and brick work is not present as a more obvious measure of age.)

However, every effort within reason has been made to offer the most accurate possible listing in the light of the circumstances outlined above.

Streets running North and South are presented in the order in which they occur if one walks west from the Potomac. Streets running from East to West are presented in the order one finds them as he approaches from Washington. In the case of each dwelling the street address is given plus a numeral denoting the number of stories and a word indicating the construction material used. The unusual flounder houses are specially noted and some of the better known dwellings are indicated by name as well.

SOUTH LEE STREET

106—2½ Story Brick
113—2 Story Brick
116—2½ Story Brick
118 " " "
120 " " "
203 " " "
205 " " "
207 " " "
208—2 Story Brick
210 " " "
212 " " "
214 " " "
209—3 Story Brick
218 " " "
219—2 Story Brick
220—2½ Story Brick Flounder
221—2 Story Wood

223—2 Story Wood
224—2½ Story Brick
307—2 Story Brick
310—2½ Story Brick
313—2 Story Brick
314—2 Story Wood
315—2½ Story Wood
316—2 Story Wood
318 " " "
401—3 Story Brick
402—2½ Stock Brick
404 " " "
406 " " "
408 " " "
410 " " "
412 " " "
403—2 Story Brick

405—2 Story Wood
407—2 Story Brick
411—2 Story Wood
418—3½ Story Brick
425—3 Story Wood
427 " " "
429—2 Story Wood
433—2½ Story Wood
435 " " "
505—3 Story Wood
509—2½ Story Brick
521 " " "
519—2 Story Wood
601—2 Story Brick
605—2½ Story Brick
615 " " "
619 " " "

NORTH FAIRFAX STREET

105—2½ Story Wood
107—3½ Story Brick
113 " " "
115 " " "
116—3 Story Brick
118—3½ Story Brick
123—2½ Story Brick (Carlyle House)

133—4 Story Brick (Bank of Alexandria)
201 " " " (John Dalton House)
208—2 Story Brick Flounder
210 " " " "
211—3 Story Brick
217 " " "
221—2½ Story Wood

SOUTH FAIRFAX STREET

105—3½ Story Brick
107 " " "
109 " " "
120—3 Story Brick
180 " " "
121 " " "
122 " " "

133—2½ Story Brick
135 " " "
137 " " "
139 " " "
203—2 Story Wood
215—2½ Story Wood
301—3½ Story Brick
307—3 Story Brick

Presbyterian Meeting House—
2 Story Brick
323—2 Story Wood
510—2½ Story Brick
514—2 Story Wood Flounder
511, 513, 515, 517—2½ Story Brick
630—2 Story Brick
625—2½ Story Wood

NORTH ROYAL STREET

111—2½ Story Brick
116—2 Story Wood
120, 122, 124—2 Story Brick

S.W. Corner of No. Royal and Cameron Sts.—3½ Story Brick
207—2 Story Wood
208—2½ Story Brick

217—3 Story Brick
219, 221—2½ Story Brick
220—3 Story Brick
300—2½ Story Wood

SOUTH ROYAL STREET

109—2½ Story Brick
112—2½ Story Wood
118—2½ Story Brick
120—2 Story Wood
122 " " "

214, 216, 218—2 Story Brick
213, 215, 217 " " "
220—2½ Story Brick
Dwelling at rear of Presbyterian Meeting House
—2½ Story Brick Flounder

NORTH PITT STREET

112—2½ Story Wood
122—2½ Story Brick
124 " " "
206—2 Story Brick
208 " " "

210—2 Story Brick
212 " " "
215—2½ Story Wood
217 " " "

219—2½ Story Wood
221 " " "
227—2 Story Wood
304—2½ Flounder

SOUTH PITT STREET

109—2½ Story Brick
110 " " "
123—2½ Story Wood
200—2½ Story Brick
202 " " "

204—3 Story Brick
206 " " "
208 " " "
210 " " "

213—3 Story Brick
229 " " "
317—2 Story Brick
319 " " "

NORTH ST. ASAPH STREET

219—2½ Story Brick

201—3 Story Brick Flounder

SOUTH ST. ASAPH STREET

113—2½ Story Brick
115 " " "
211—3 Story Brick

301—3 Story Brick (Lafayette House)
305—2½ Story Brick
307—3 Story Brick

310—3 Story Brick
317—2 Story Brick Flounder

NORTH WASHINGTON STREET

128—SE Corner Princess
  3 Story Brick
215—3½ Story Brick
220—2½ Story Brick

301—3 Story Wood
303 " " "
305 " " "

307—3 Story Wood
329—3 Story Brick
428—2½ Story Brick

SOUTH WASHINGTON STREET

201—SW Corner Prince, 2 Story
  Brick (Lyceum)
209—2 Story Brick
220—2½ Story Brick
222—3 Story Brick
224 " " "
226 " " "

228—3 Story Brick
230 " " "
312—2½ Story Brick
314 " " "
401—2 Story Wood
403 " " "
405 " " "

407—2 Story Wood
409 " " "
411 " " "
413—2½ Story Brick
415 " " "
SE Corner Wolfe—3 Story
  Brick School

COLUMBUS STREET

SE Corner Cameron—Christ Church
111—2½ Story Brick
113—2 Story Brick Flounder
119—2 Story Brick
211—2 Story Wood
217—2½ Story Brick

506—2 Story Brick
508 " " "
510 " " "
512 " " "
514 " " "
516 " " "

518—2 Story Brick
520 " " "
610 " " "
614 " " "
616 " " "   Flounder

NORTH ALFRED STREET

105—3 Story Brick
107—Engine House
112—2 Story Brick
114 " " "
115 " " "

116—2½ Story Brick
122—2 Story Brick Flounder
224—2 Story Brick
226 " " "

300—2 Story Brick
302 " " "
304 " " "
306—2 Story Wood

SOUTH ALFRED STREET

112—2 Story Brick
114 " " "

116—2 Story Brick
115—2½ Story Brick

117—2 Story Brick

ORONOCO STREET

SE Corner Washington—3 Story Wood   607—2½ Story Brick   609—2½ Story Brick

PRINCESS STREET

711—2½ Story Brick (Open center hall type)

QUEEN STREET

116—2 Story Brick
118 " " "
124 " " "
126 " " "
215 " " "
217 " " "
310—2 Story Wood
312—2 Story Brick
316—2 Story Wood
320 " " "
322 " " "
324 " " "
326 " " "
328 " " "
317—3 Story Brick

319—2 Story Brick
321 " " "
323 " " "
325 " " "
306—2 Story Wood
308 " " "
310 " " "
316 " " "
320 " " "
322 " " "
324 " " "
326 " " "
328 " " "
403 " " "

405—2 Story Wood
407 " " "
409 " " "
411 " " "
413 " " "
601—3 Story Brick
603 " " "
609—2½ Story Brick
611 " " "
904—2 Story Brick
906 " " "
918 " " "
920 " " "
922 " " "

CAMERON STREET

211—2 Story Brick
303—3½ Story Brick
305—2½ Story Brick
311—3 Story Brick
313—2½ Story Brick
323—3 Story Brick
325 " " "
501 " " "

502—2 Story Brick
504 " " "
505 " " "
506—3 Story Brick
507—2 Story Wood
509—2 Story Brick
511—2½ Story Brick

602—3 Story Brick
Lord Fairfax House—3 Story Brick
609—2½ Story Brick
611 " " "
606 " " "
608 " " "
912 " " "

KING STREET

SE Corner Union—3 Story Brick
111—3 Story Brick
113 " " "
115 " " "
117 " " "
119 " " "
201 " " "
207—2 Story Brick
208—3 Story Brick
213 " " "
217 " " "
210—2 Story Brick
300—3 Story Brick
328 " " "
400 " " "
404 " " "
416—2 Story Brick
418 " " "
420 " " "
430—3 Story Brick
431 " " "

519—3½ Story Brick
521 " " "
520 " " "
522 " " "
SE Corner St. Asaph—3 Story Brick
NE " Washington—3½ Story Brick
SE " " " " "
701—3½ Story Brick
707 " " "
711 " " "
713 " " "
715 " " "
717 " " "
807 " " "
900—2 Story Brick
904 " " "
907—3 Story Brick
915—3½ Story Brick
917 " " "
919 " " "
921 " " "

918—3 Story Brick
920 " " "
922 " " "
924—3½ Story Brick
1007—2½ Story Brick
1011 " " "
1102 " " "
1104 " " "
1106 " " "
1122—2 Story Brick
1124 " " "
1201—3 Story Brick
1225 " " "
1229—2½ Story Brick
1302—2 Story Brick
1303—2 Story Wood
1305—2 Story Brick
1315 " " "
1316—3 Story Brick
1319—2 Story Brick
1322 " " "

PRINCE STREET

Corner Union St.—two 3 Story Brick
103—2 Story Brick
105 " " "
107 " " "
106—2½ Story Brick
108 " " "
109—2 Story Brick
111 " " "

113—2 Story Brick
114 " " "
115—3 Story Brick
116—3½ Story Brick
118 " " "
117—3 Story Brick
119 " " "
121—2 Story Brick

123—2 Story Brick
127—3 Story Brick
128—2 Story Wood
130 " " "
200—3 Story Brick
207—3½ Story Brick
209 " " "
210 " " "

PRINCE STREET—(Continued)

211—3½ Story Brick
213 " " "
215 " " "
212—3½ Story Wood
214 " " "
216—3½ Story Brick
217—2 Story Wood
302—2½ Story Brick
305—3½ Story Brick
309—2½ Story Brick
311 " " "
SW Corner Royal Street—
    2½ Story Brick
413—3½ Story Brick
504—2 Story Brick
506—2½ Story Brick

517—1½ Story Wood
520—3½ Story Brick
803—3 Story Brick
804 " " "
808 " " "
817—2 Story Brick
819 " " "
905—3 Story Brick
916 " " "
1004 " " "
1010—2½ Story Brick
1012 " " "
1014—3 Story Brick
1016—2 Story Brick
1020—2½ Story Brick

1101—2½ Story Brick
1103 " " "
1105 " " "
1107 " " "
1108 " " "
1110 " " "
1111 " " "
1112 " " "
1113 " " "
1114 " " "
1115 " " "
1117 " " "
1201—2 Story Brick
1208 " " "
1210 " " "

DUKE STREET

109—2 Story Brick
121—3 Story Brick
123 " " "
125 " " "
200—2 Story Wood
201—2½ Story Wood
202—2½ Story Brick Flounder
205—2 Story Brick Flounder
211—2 Story Wood
210—3½ Story Brick
212—2½ Story Wood
300—3 Story Wood
306—2 Story Wood

308—2 Story Wood
311—2 Story Brick
314 " " "
316 " " "
318 " " "
321 " " "
323—2½ Story Wood
325 " " "
404—3½ Story Brick
408—3 Story Brick
417—2 Story Brick
515, 519—2½ Story Wood

521—2½ Story Brick
601 " " "
    (Dulaney House)
620—3 Story Brick
700—2½ Story Brick
805—3 Story Wood
902—2 Story Wood
904 " " "
1001—2 Story Brick
1009 " " "
1123—2½ Story Brick
1207 " " "

WOLFE STREET

106—2 Story Wood
114—2½ Story Wood
116 " " "
118 " " "
120 " " "
123—2 Story Wood
125 " " "
127 " " "
205 " " "

207—2 Story Wood
209 " " "
211 " " "
216—2 Story Brick
221—2 Story Wood
311—2 Story Brick
313 " " "
315 " " "

317—2 Story Brick
406—2 Story Wood
411—2 Story Brick
706—2 Story Wood
714—2 Story Brick
800 " " "
801 " " "
803 " " "

WILKES STREET

413—2 Story Brick

GIBBON STREET

207—2½ Story Brick
209 " " "

217—2 Story Brick
221—3 Story Brick

FRANKLIN STREET

800—2 Story Brick
802 " " "
814—2 Story Wood (Jockey Club)

815—1½ Story Wood (Arch Hall)
816—2 Story Brick

818—2 Story Brick
900, 920—2 Story Brick

JEFFERSON STREET

215—2½ Story Brick